For John, my beloved

And for my mother,
who asks me every year if I am a Christian.
I wish I had a shorter answer to that question than this.

CONTENTS

PREFACE

This is a story about the kingdom of heaven and one man's search for it, starting in the Southern Baptist Church into which he was born. One gay man's search, I might add, since sexual orientation is important to the story. One gay man's successful search, I might also add, by way of letting the reader know ahead of time that this story has a happy ending.

Like any memoir, this book is a record of the past. Yet the fact is that the past does not exist. What exists are memories, and memories are thoughts that, like all thoughts, rise through the void of the mind like plants growing toward sunlight from the bottom of a pond. When thoughts come to light in the mind of God, he arranges them into a pattern we call "the universe." When thoughts arise and blossom in our own minds, we arrange them into patterns as well. We arrange thoughts about things around us into a story we call "the world." Thoughts about ourselves we arrange into a story we call "me." The apostles Matthew, Mark, Luke and John arranged thoughts about Jesus into stories we call Gospels. Jesus arranged his thoughts into one simple message that he spread as far as he could in his brief life: the kingdom of heaven is here, on earth, right now. The trick is in learning to see it. Once seen, what the seer beholds is nothing less than the mind of God.

"Whoever does not express his gratitude to people will never be grateful to God." If you guessed Jesus, you are not far off the mark—the words are those of the next prophet, Muhammad. The following people have my unending gratitude for their suggestions and support in the writing of this book: my mother, Jane Austin; my partner, John Dunn (yes, I know, I know); my friends Rolf Schelander, Simone Bloch-Wehba, Peter Reynaud, Anthony Korf, Garth Pritchard, Diane Barclay and Jacklyn Johnston; my friend and agent, Helen Shabason; and my friend and lifelong teacher, Kent Cathcart. Thanks as well go to the Missionary Sisters of the Immaculate Heart of Mary for being such an appreciative audience. I also owe a tremendous debt of gratitude to my friends Roger Miller, Gaye Sandler, Barbara Dubitsky and Brucie Barrett—liberal humanists all—for their looks of thunderstruck wonder the evening I let drop, for the first time in over thirty years, that I am a born-again Christian. This book had its genesis in those looks, and in the shower of questions that followed, on that beautiful summer evening at Tom and Ulla Atkinson's cabin overlooking Lost Lake.

New York City, New York

THE THOUSAND-PETALED LOTUS

Growing up Gay in the Southern Baptist Church

A MEMOIR

MICHAEL FIELDS

When I was eleven years old, I gave my life to Jesus.

I have no reason to think that he ever gave it back.

PROLOGUE

THE MIND OF GOD

One hardly knows where to begin.

Start at the beginning.

Born February 6, 1956, Nashville, Tennessee. Born again August 15, 1967, baptized the following Sunday at Grace Baptist Church, Nashville, Tennessee. Died to self October 20, 2007, Bally's Gym, Sixth Avenue at Twentieth Street, New York City, New York.

In the eternal mind of God, all those fine beginnings are happening right now, at this very moment. The dilemma for a metaphysically minded memoirist should be immediately apparent.

Start again.

We think of eternity as infinite time, as one endless day of heavenly bliss (or blistering hellfire) that lasts forever. That is the common hope—or fear, as the case may be. But suppose God does not see it that way. Suppose that when God looks out on creation, suppose that when he looks out on your life, or mine, he sees no time at all, infinite or otherwise. Suppose that, for the eternal God, eternity has nothing to do with time. There are other definitions of eternity. Here is one I like: existence outside of time. By this definition, God, who is limitless in every dimension including the fourth, exists outside time altogether.

Which still leaves me wondering where to begin. Where would God start my story, or yours, if for him every starting point is the same?

Start again. Where God starts.

In the beginning God created heaven and earth. It took him six days. Consider that it takes Santa Claus all year to make the toys that Christian children demand for Christmas. Three hundred sixty-five days for Santa versus six days for God.

If there were a being whose greatness stood in relation to God's, as God's does to Santa's, how quickly could the earth have been made? Might God's supervisor have done it in six hours? Six minutes? Six seconds?

What the Bible account of creation fails to mention is that the eternal God created time before he made heaven and earth. Otherwise we would not know how long it took him to make anything else.

Start again. In the beginning …

Time is a created thing. God created it for our use, not his. God, being eternal, has no need for time. Let us not quibble then about how long it took God to make heaven and earth. It took no time at all. Why would it?

Consider creation. How long does it take to make a thing, a simple thing, a hamburger, for instance? Cooking the burger, slicing the tomatoes and setting out the condiments takes approximately thirty minutes, if one is not distracted. God is not distracted, so how long does it take God to make a hamburger? The Bible says that God made cattle on the sixth day. Since he rested on the seventh, it is safe to assume that the creation of condiments had to wait until Monday. A creationist, then, would have to give God several days to make a hamburger, at least back then. On the other hand, a secular humanist would have to allow God billions of years just to make solid matter, much less anything to eat. But let us say that today God, having created heaven and earth billions and billions of years ago—or maybe just three or four thousand years ago, depending on whose book you like—now wishes to make a hamburger. How long would it take? He doesn't have to shop for it or cook it, like we do. All God has to do is think of a hamburger and then there is a hamburger. The process happens in an instant. First there is the thought and immediately upon completion of the thought, there is the burger.

Except that God created time for our use, not his. What is one to think, therefore, about the instant that it takes God to make a hamburger? Is it a long instant or a short instant? Is it a moment or a nanosecond? If we grant that God is eternal and that eternity is existence outside of time, then it should take God no time at all to make a hamburger. There is no thought of a burger followed instantly by the burger itself. There is only thought/burger. God's thought does not become a hamburger; God's thought about the hamburger *is* the hamburger. The thought is the burger. The burger is the thought. They are one and the same thing. Now substitute the word "universe" for the word "hamburger" wherever it is used in this paragraph and think what that means. The universe is both thought and reality in the mind of God, as surely as that hamburger is.

As surely as we are.

PART ONE

BIG CHURCH

*S*tart again. *At the beginning.*

Born February 6, 1956.

The first Christmas I remember was in 1958, when I was two years old. Some may think that we do not retain memories from such an early age, but I know otherwise. My family moved to the house in which I would grow up, at 2900 Rich Acres Drive, in April 1959, which means that every memory I have of life in my parents' first house on Dearborn Drive was of a time when I was barely three years old or, in the case of Christmas 1958, not even that. My earliest memory is of the door between the den and the bedroom hall in that first house—or to put it more accurately, of the doorknob on that door. My parents were attempting to herd me into the living room to see my presents on Christmas morning when I suddenly realized that the penny I was carrying might just fit into the keyhole of that doorknob. I did not know what a "present" was and had to be pried away from the door. My next memory of that Christmas is of playing with my favorite present, a gas station with a parking lot on the roof where I could park all the toy cars I received that year.

Cars were my favorite things. I could name them all as they came down the street, and I had a fleet of toy cars that I put under my pillow every night. The gas station only magnified my delight in the cars. It had a ramp that led from an opening in the roof, down through the interior of the building to a doorway in the side. I spent Christmas morning of 1958 tipping my cars down the ramp on the gas station roof and watching them shoot out the door below. That such a thing was possible was beyond my comprehension. How could it be? I put the car in up here; it comes out down there. I put the car in up here; it comes out down there. I could not figure it out. When I finally asked my father how this wonder worked, he turned the gas station around to show me that the back was completely open. As I looked into the gas station from the back, my father tipped a car onto the ramp above. I watched in amazement as the car whizzed down the ramp through the gas station. I spent Christmas afternoon watching my cars whiz down that ramp. And herein can be found a lesson that explains the different positions occupied by humans and animals on the Great Chain of Being. My aunt Peggy once had a cat who enjoyed watching baseball on television. Every time a batter hit the ball and broke for first, the cat would run behind the television set to see where he went. I learned where the cars went and by Christmas night had lost interest in my gas station. The cat never figured out where the runners went and remained a lifelong fan of baseball. Is it any wonder, then, that on the sixth day, it was man who was allowed to name the animals and not the other way around?

Other early memories:

My father carrying me through the woods at the back of our yard to watch the train pass.

Standing beside my bed, shaking my piggy bank when I was supposed to be taking a nap, wanting to know how much money I had but unable to shake the coins out of the narrow slot. My mother coming in when she heard all the racket, showing me the rubber stopper on the bottom of the bank. My coins spread out on the bed. It did not look like much money to me.

Riding in the backseat of the blue-and-white Chevrolet station wagon on the way to my grandmother Nanny's house on Stainback Avenue. Trying to understand who this person was that we were on our way to see. My parents in the front seat, explaining what a cousin is. My dazzling aunt Peggy sitting on the piano bench at Nanny's house, dangling Ricky by his hands so that his feet just touched the floor. Ricky grinning at us, so pleased at the prospect of standing on his own someday. His close-cropped hair so white he looked bald.

Other Mother's canary in the bungalow on Meridian Street. The red house down the block where my grandparents, Bee Pa and Mama Fields, lived with my great-great-aunt Kate and my aunt Annelle. Aunt Kate playing the grand piano that filled the front room of the house. I understood that all these greats and others and aunts were related to me but struggled to understand how they were related to each other.

Protesting as the nurse took away my balloon as I was wheeled on the gurney to the operating room. The metal cone that was lowered over my face when the ether was administered. Grown-ups I had seen at church standing in the doorway to my hospital room, holding toy cars instead of flowers, having no doubt prayed for me after seeing my name listed in the church bulletin that Sunday as a child in need of special prayers. Who could have easily died when he complained of a stomachache, had his parents not rushed him to a doctor who ordered the swift removal of his appendix.

Sitting on the porch swing at Nanny's house with my family, seeing Nanny come out of the gray bungalow wearing her nightgown in the middle of the afternoon and not understanding why. No one would have mentioned cancer to a three-year-old. Nanny, forty-one years old, with three grandchildren of whom I was the oldest, the one who named her "Nanny" because I could not say "Granny." When we were old enough to understand, she would tell her grandchildren how her doctors in the hospital had told her she would not live through the night, and how she had prayed that God would let her live to see us grown. One much later memory, my last of my grandmother: Nanny lying in a hospital bed, smiling and reaching out to Collin, her great-grandson, who was the same age that day as I was on Nanny's porch, thirty-six years before.

Most of my early memories are of struggling to make sense of the world. One day I noticed something odd about the pattern of bricks on the patio across which I was hurtling on my tricycle. All I saw was an expanse of brick that I intended to pedal across, yet something was different about the bricks at the end of the patio where my father was leaping out of his chair and my mother was crying out for me to stop. It was not until I was airborne that I remembered my father had built one end of our patio a foot lower than the other. By the time my father scooped his bawling heir off the patio, I had learned something new about the world: if one thing looks different from another thing, it probably is.

Except when it isn't. One day I was playing alone in the front yard (a feat unimaginable in today's world of supervised play), when I spied a huge striped beast creeping along the hedge. The beast stopped, turned its head, and gazed at me with enormous golden eyes. I was transfixed. I wanted to run, but my feet would not move. I did not know what this creature was. It looked like pictures I had seen of cats, but those cats were small creatures curled around the ankles of children who were much older than I. This thing was as big as I was, which meant it looked different from the illustrations of cats and must therefore be another thing. The only image in my memory that offered any clue to this creature's identity was an illustration in a book I had, called *Little Black Sambo*. When the creature released me from its gaze and continued its slow creep along the hedge, I ran into the house and told my mother there was a tiger in the yard. I did not know what "your imagination" was and thereafter checked the yard for tigers whenever I went outside. That continued until the day my father backed a rented truck into the driveway, and I watched as he, my uncle J. K. and my twelve-year-old cousin David loaded our furniture into the back of it. I was allowed to ride in the cab with them to our new house on Rich Acres Drive, where I would learn more new things until the world started to make some sense. One of the first things I learned on Rich Acres Drive was that the tall man who lived in the big brick ranch house that I could see from the picture window in our living room was the same man who stood in the pulpit at Grace Baptist Church every Sunday, shouting something about a place called hell.

The new house at 2900 Rich Acres Drive was a modest brick ranch on one acre of land, with three bedrooms that my parents needed after the birth of my sister, Kim. Like the other houses in the neighborhood, it was smaller than the parsonage at the top of the hill but not for long. Soon after moving in, my parents made their first addition—a one-car garage to replace the original garage they had annexed to create a family room, or "den," as we called it then. The den was paneled in the early American style and was furnished with a suite of blond wood furniture upholstered in white Naugahyde. Since the original heating system of the house did not extend to the den, a heater with metal coils was built into the wall near the floor. Any parent reading this will recognize our peril immediately. My parents recognized it soon enough. One day when Kim and I were two and four, respectively, we invented a new sport. The sport involved throwing a piece of paper into the metal coils of the heater and then running one lap around the sofa while the paper burst into flames. We were just about to give our new sport a name when our mother smelled smoke. Our Olympic dream died when she charged into the room, lightning flashing from her aqua-colored eyes. Most of what I know about fire today I learned in the tirade that lasted the next five minutes. The house was never again threatened by fire and continued to grow. The birth of my brother, Miles, and increasing demand for my father's services as a freelance illustrator resulted in the addition of a dining room, a larger kitchen, a dinette balcony overlooking a new family room, and a large new bedroom on the back of the house with a private pink bathroom for my parents.

That our house had finally reached the size of the parsonage did not escape the notice of our pastor. Brother Lindsay figured that no house in that working-class neighborhood could double in size in a few short years without God having a hand in it somehow. He asked my father to be one of several guest speakers drawn from the congregation who would precede the sermon one Sunday night by sharing a personal story about a miracle that God had worked for them. There was nothing miraculous about my father's story to start. Standing in the pulpit, he confessed that he had always intended to save money on our additions by finishing up the interiors himself once the contractor had put on the roof. The men in the congregation nodded their approval of a young man who was handy with tools. My father then went on to tell how, in his zeal to finish the additions, he had stopped illustrating altogether and devoted himself full time to carpentry. That would have been bad enough for our finances had he not also gotten carried away with his embellishments. My parents wanted a beamed ceiling in their new family room and dinette. Not content to tack up some fake beams and call it a day, my father actually constructed the ceiling out of heavy beams that he had carefully distressed with a blowtorch so that the room looked as though it had been there for a hundred and fifty years. He was then unable to stop himself when, after stripping the streamlined kitchen cabinets and refurbishing them in early American style, he felt the need to adorn the area over the stove with a handmade wooden hood, topped off with a carving of an American eagle holding three arrows and a shield painted with the stars and stripes of the American flag. When he finally set aside his hammer, saw and chisels, we had a unique and beautiful house. We were also close to ruin. My father had not taken any work in months. One night after we sat down to dinner, my father told his children that things would be tight for a while and not to expect much in the way of new toys or candy until God sent us some money. Then he bowed his head and asked the blessing, a task that in our house was ordinarily reserved for a child. To the usual request that God bless our bodies with nourishment from our food, he tacked on another request for work. Within a month, my father told the congregation, he had received over a thousand dollars worth of work. Even in that staid congregation, a couple of the men said "Amen." I had listened to the whole story from the pews and almost burst with pride at the conclusion. My father was the only guest speaker that night who put a dollar value on God's love. In 1966, a thousand dollars was ample proof that God loved the Fields family very much indeed.

God loved the Fields family so much that He could not bear for us to be more than a few short blocks away from each other. We had been on Rich Acres only a few months and our house was still small when the red bungalow on Meridian was sold to make way for a store. Mama Fields, Bee Pa, Annelle and Aunt Kate moved to a pink brick house that had just been built three blocks from our own. Aunt Kate passed away soon after, the grand piano was sold and my great-grandmother, who was never called anything but Other Mother, took her place. Only Nanny remained in the old neighborhood in town, where there were sidewalks, streetlights, sewers and only a dozen feet between one house and the next. My father had grown up in that neighborhood, in a house two blocks away from Grace Baptist Church. The house Nanny bought was two blocks from the church in the other direction, on Stainback just off Douglas Avenue. That was where my father, thirteen years old and wheeling around the corner one day from Douglas onto Stainback, nearly wrecked his bicycle the first time he saw my mother—tiny, blonde and newly moved up from Cleveland, Tennessee—stepping out onto the porch of her new home.

My mother spent most of her time ironing clothes and cooking, which were activities she could do while watching soap operas. Watching soap operas seemed to me like a good use of a mother's time. There was one that I liked myself. Every afternoon, I, who could barely tell time, would somehow know that the best way to occupy myself at that moment was to go inside and sit on the floor between the ironing board and the television set to watch *The Secret Storm*. After several weeks of this, my mother remarked, "I believe you must like Kip." I agreed that I did. As soon as I'd said it, I felt embarrassed. For some reason I did not want to talk about my interest in the strangely magnetic young man on the television screen. One day when I took my seat in front of the ironing board, I got confused. There was a new character on the show. All the other characters kept calling him Kip, but he was not Kip. I asked my mother what had happened, and she said that a new actor was now playing the role of Kip. This new actor was not strangely magnetic. I returned to *The Secret Storm* every afternoon for a week before I finally accepted that the old Kip was not coming back. I abandoned the new Kip to the old Kip's problems and went back outside to play. Doing that gave me a certain sense of relief, as I had begun to sense even then that it was somehow not okay to show too much interest in a handsome soap opera character.

The same did not apply to the Rifleman. It was okay to watch *The Rifleman* because he carried a gun—and not just any gun. While the other gunslingers would whip out a paltry pistol from their holsters in the gun duels that climaxed every episode, Lucas McCain would haul out a rifle that he had specially modified so that he could aim it while keeping it slung low, down by his narrow hips. He could cock and fire the rifle in one smooth, swift motion of his hand and never failed to fill his guest stars with bullets. I was in love, all the more so because Lucas McCain was also a single father. Every week just before the credit roll, he would sit his boy, Mark, on his knee and together they would rejoice that the Rifleman had lived another day to sit with his boy on his knee.

I did not know that I was gay when I was born, but I am sure that I was. God makes homosexuals as surely as he makes everything else. One has to believe this unless one tricks oneself into believing that homosexuals snuck into creation through some back door in the universe that God forgot to lock on his way out. I once tested the "nurture" side of the "nature or nurture" debate about the origins of homosexuality by blaming my sexual orientation on my parents. I was unable to sustain that fantasy for more than a few days. It simply crumpled under the weight of evidence to the contrary. My first crush happened long before my parents recognized what was happening or could do anything to aid and abet or quash it. I did not know it was a crush at the time, of course. All I knew was that if I whined and pleaded and carried on long enough,

I could have any comic book that featured J'onn J'onzz, the Martian Manhunter. The Martian Manhunter was green and bald and had big muscles, most of which were fully revealed by a costume that was nothing more than a blue cape and boots, a blue bikini bottom and two red straps that crisscrossed his manly chest. There was nothing that magnetized me more than the sight of that green beefcake flying across the cover of a comic book. I wanted to be more like Jesus, the way everyone told me I should be, but what I really wanted was a blue cape, a set of red straps across my chest, and permission to fly around the world hunting for men with J'onn J'onzz. I had the good sense to keep this fantasy to myself, somehow sensing, even at that young age, that these strange feelings for the Martian Manhunter were of a rare and pure kind that would only be trampled upon in Sunday school.

My mother spent her days ironing clothes and cooking while she watched soap operas. I spent my days trying to fly off the end of our picnic table in a Superman suit that I pestered my parents into ordering for me out of the Sears catalog one Christmas. Outside of learning to fly, my favorite activities included climbing trees, pestering my sister, and throwing rocks at Dennis and Cathy, the little imps who lived across the street. My mother paid scant attention to me, which worked out just fine for her because apparently there was a little bird who flew into the kitchen all day long to recite all the sins I was committing out in the yard. I was too young to realize that the little bird was probably Jesus, when one afternoon, after hearing about that little bird for what I was determined would be the last time, I set out into the yard with my sling-shot. I never found the little bird and anyway, I couldn't hit the broad side of a barn with a slingshot. Every time I failed to kill something with it, I thought about David and Goliath and how the whole history of the world would have been different if I had been on that battlefield instead of David. I also thought about how interesting it would be if my playmates and I wore short little tunics like the one David wore in my illustrated Bible.

My favorite picture in my illustrated Bible was the one of Goliath crumpling before the victorious David. Which is a picture of a boy in a frock with a muscular older man. Do people really see what they are looking at? Lucas McCain with his hand slung down by his hip, cocking his rifle over and over; a near-naked superhero whose sole purpose is the pursuit of men; David launching a rock at a man in uniform?

In the beginning God created heaven and earth. Of what did he create them? What material was available to him (or her) then? If the only given in the beginning was God, then we can only think that God must have created heaven and earth out of himself, there being no other substance existing before the invention of time. We might also say that God created heaven and earth out of nothing, but that might lead us to conclude that God himself is nothing.

In the beginning God created heaven and earth. Of what material did he create them? What material was available to him when all was darkness and void? Let us say for the sake of argument that God decides that he wants to make a universe, or a hamburger. Or a homosexual. Yes, let us imagine that God wishes to make a homosexual. Just for laughs, if that's all we think homosexuals are good for. Or because the road to hell needs another paving stone, if that's what we think God thinks homosexuals are good for. The one thing we can be sure of here is that homosexuals must be good for something since God turns them out by the wagonload.

There are good folks everywhere who have little use for homosexuals, and plenty of others who have no use for them at all, who appear to regard homosexuals as some sort of mistake. Conservative estimates put the ratio of homos to heteros at somewhere around one to twenty, or approximately 5 percent of the population. If homosexuals are a mistake, that means that God's margin for error is plus or minus 5 percent. I would prefer that God have no margin for error at all, since God is the sole creator of the universe through which, for better or worse, I must make my way. As you must, as well.

Other than one trip to Dallas when I was four years old to visit my father's oldest sister Jean, my uncle Raymond, and my older cousins David and Sharon, the only place we ever went was Cleveland, Tennessee. Every summer, my mother would organize a trip to the town in southern Tennessee where she'd lived with her grandmother Susie until she was thirteen. Today the trip can be made by car in a little more than two hours. Back then we had to get up early in the morning to make the trip because it took all day, or at least it felt so. We would begin the trip at Parker's Market three blocks from our house, where my parents bought comic books that kept Kim and me quiet only for the thirty miles to Murfreesboro because neither of us could read. After that I sat with my cheek against the window, looking out at mile after mile of farms, waiting for the billboards that announced our distance from the wonders of Ruby Falls and Rock City and Lookout Mountain, none of which we ever stopped to see. After lunch at a redwood, stone and glass restaurant in Monteagle, my father would put the car into second gear for the steep descent on the two-lane highway that hugged the side of the mountain as we climbed down off the Cumberland plateau toward Chattanooga. The time it took to get to the house on Walker Street no longer mattered once I saw Susie waving to us from the porch that was no more than eight feet from the street. She always looked the same as she hugged us and led us into the house—stoop-shouldered, wearing a floral print house dress, her long, gray hair braided and coiled and held in place at the nape of her neck by two brown plastic combs.

The dark front door of Susie's house, with its two arched windows, was a portal back to my mother's childhood and to my grandmother's as well. My great-grandfather, John Henry Collins, died before Nanny was born. Susie went to work sewing pockets onto men's trousers at a woolen mill and never had money to spend on her house beyond making the most basic repairs. By the time I was born, the paint had mostly peeled off the clapboards and the exposed wood was weathered gray. One end of the back room had sunk almost a foot from level. The house had two black coal stoves, one in the kitchen and one in the front room, that Susie would light on cold mornings. An old washing machine with a hand-cranked wringer on top stood in a corner of the dining room where every night around the claw-foot oval table we ate fried chicken and biscuits and gravy and mashed potatoes and corn on the cob. The rooms of Susie's house were dark and high-ceilinged and arranged in no particular order. Outside it was much the same. The extra lot Susie owned next to the house was a paradise of wild strawberries and roses and peonies and overgrown hedges full of hiding places where we played all day until the bottoms of our feet were black and our necks were ringed with dirt. After dinner, Susie would heat water in kettles to fill the claw-foot tub that stood in the bathroom at the end of a long screened porch where her dead husband's tools lay rusting in the humid air. After our baths, we kids would be put to bed in the front bedroom, where we fell asleep to the sound of cars passing down the street just outside the open window, their headlamps casting beams of light through the thin lace curtains and across the iron headboard and around the dark walls of my favorite place on earth.

Mornings and evenings in Cleveland we sat with Susie on her front porch. Afternoons we visited relatives. My favorite afternoon every year was the one we spent on Peoples Street visiting my maternal grandfather's family, the Fowlers. We did not visit my maternal grandfather himself because Bud Fowler was killed in a car accident when my mother was a baby. The Fowlers owned the better part of Peoples Street, or so it seemed to me when I was a child. At the house on the corner that my great-grandmother shared with her sister Hattie, Granny Fowler would ask us kids how we were and then give us each a peppermint candy that we would suck on the porch while our parents visited inside. Across the street, Mother's aunt Ruby would ask us how we were and then give us each a pickle she had put up that winter. We got nothing to eat at the house of Mother's cousin Grace next door since we had already climbed halfway up the maple trees out front before our parents crossed the porch. When we were exhausted and starting to get cranky, our parents would send us across the street and watch from Grace's porch as we swarmed into a tiny white-frame grocery store that stood on the corner. The store belonged to Granny Fowler and was run by her son Russell. Because we were family, we were allowed to have two items each for free. Russell would smile at each of us from the cash register as we walked past with a Moon Pie in one hand and a soda in the other. With no parents there to supervise, we chose sodas that we would never get at home, Dr. Pepper or Nehi Grape or Orange Crush. How I loved that store!

What I loved best was the sound that the screen door made as it slammed shut behind me when I carried my treasures out to the sidewalk. Once the treats were consumed, we had just enough time to pay a quick call on Mother's aunt Mary Ruth around the corner before the sugar rush kicked in, at which time we were whisked off to the home of Mother's cousin Marlene. There we finished the afternoon playing in the basement with our second cousin Sandy and her telepathic twin sisters Pamela and Tamera.

The Fowlers date back to the sixth day of creation. So does everyone else, but the Fowlers can prove it. Fifteen years ago, my mother assembled her grown children and her four-year-old grandson, Collin, for what might have been my last trip to Cleveland. The occasion was a family reunion organized by Mother's cousins Judy and Beulah Mae. We rode down from Nashville on the day before the reunion in a Cadillac piloted by my mother's second husband, Jim. My mother chatted happily the whole way. She was particularly excited by Judy's promise that the family tree she had been researching for several years would be distributed to everyone at the covered-dish luncheon that would take place in the basement of the church where the Fowlers worshipped.

On the day of the reunion, Jim parked the car among many others in a gravel parking lot behind the North Cleveland Church of God. Gathered there that Saturday afternoon were people I had not seen in twenty years—great-aunts and great-uncles grown old, second cousins with children of their own, and many other people I had never met, including one charming young man who drove over from the motel where he and his family were living after their house was flattened by a tornado from which they had barely escaped alive. The only thing that marred my mother's joy that day was Judy's announcement that her genealogy was not quite finished. My mother took what Judy had written so far and agreed to proofread it. That arrangement went on, year after eye-straining year, as Judy went deeper and deeper into the past and sent the results of her research up to Nashville to be proofed. One night on the telephone, my mother told me that Judy had at last found royalty in our blood, a tenth-century German king named Henry the Fowler.

"Wow," I said, "Judy's traced us all the way back to the Dark Ages."

"*Dark Ages?*" my mother shot back. "Mike, she has traced us back to the *Bible!*"

Several years later I received a package in the mail that contained my completed, bound copy of the genealogy. It was two inches thick. I took a moment to leaf through the tome, starting from the back as I always do, pausing here and there just to see how far back in history I had traveled. I glanced with interest at the section on the Trojan War before leafing back to another page that started off with the words "The Caucasian race began ..." When I had leafed all the way back to page one, I glanced at the top and sure enough, there they were: Adam of Eden and his wife, Eve. No wonder Judy wasn't ready to publish in time for the family reunion. My mother complained about it after the luncheon as we climbed into the Cadillac. Most of the Fowlers had left by then, and the car stood alone in the parking lot at one end of a block that had been completely leveled—bought up by the burgeoning Church of God—save for one old house and two enormous maple trees. I did not know where we were until my mother said, "That's Grace's house. She won't sell, not even to her own church. Everything else is gone." Everything else was indeed gone, or going. Hauled up onto the back of a flatbed truck was the only other building in sight, a small white-frame structure with a blackened screen door. It was Granny Fowler's store.

The past does not exist. What exists are memories. Memories are thoughts, and thoughts exist only now. When God looks at the world, he sees it *now.* God has no future. Why would God ever have to wait for anything? God has no past. Why would he ever have to give anything up? From God's point of view, the moment of recognizing your great-grandmother's store on the back of a truck is the same moment the screen door slams shut behind you as you tear off down the street, a Moon Pie in one hand and an Orange Crush in the other, a smile on your face and on the face of your mother who watches from her cousin's porch and sees her childhood mirrored in your own as the great Mobius strip of space/time loops back on itself, memory lapped over the present moment, all one moment in the eternal mind of God.

In the beginning, God. Here are the things I learned about God at Grace Baptist Church:

1. God exists. Atheists go to hell.
2. God created heaven and earth. God created hell, too, but not in that first week since he had no one to send there until the end of the second.
3. God is omnipresent, omnipotent and omniscient.
4. God is perfect, which is not quite the same thing as #3, above. My mother was omnipresent and omniscient (with her little bird's help) but fell just short of perfection.
5. God lives in heaven, which is not anywhere around here. God can be coaxed to leave heaven and pay one a visit anytime through prayer.
6. When something bad happens, that is called God's will. When something good happens, that is called luck and we must thank God for it.
7. God loves the United States of America more than any other country in the world except for Israel. He is also fond of England and would like Canada as well if he ever thought about it.
8. God loves all his children equally, but he is fair about it. This means that:
   a. Catholics go to hell.
   b. Jews go to hell.
   c. Hindus go to hell.
   d. Muslims go to hell.

e. Buddhists go to hell.

f. Little children who die before they reach the age of accountability go to heaven. The age of accountability is the age at which a child knows right from wrong and can therefore be held responsible for his actions, hereinafter called "sins." The exact age of accountability is not specified. It seems to vary from child to child. It also varies from parent to parent, who often sustain a belief in a child's innocence long past the time when everyone else starts praying for his salvation.

9. Despite the fairness clause in *8b,* above, it is a known fact that God loves the Jews more than he loves anyone else, because they are his chosen people. He therefore regrets any inconvenience that may be caused by sending them all to hell.

10. God is merciful. Anyone in the world can avoid the fires of hell (as I have done) by accepting Jesus Christ as his personal Lord and Savior. Salvation takes only a few minutes. It is also free, unless you think of giving your life to Jesus as a cost. The trick is to find out about salvation before you die and go to hell. That people do die all over the world every day without ever hearing about salvation through Jesus Christ is a heavy burden on the hearts of Southern Baptists. Baptists are therefore careful to donate money every year through the Lottie Moon Christmas Offering to support the work of missionaries in the hope that there will someday be enough

missionaries to reach every lost soul in the world before it dies.

11. Whether God's mercy extends to homosexuals is not a question that could be answered, as it is not a question that could be asked. The love that dare not speak its name was certainly never spoken of at Grace Baptist Church.

Grace Baptist Church was founded in 1910. Over the next fifty years, Grace, like most other mainline Christian churches, grew rapidly in membership until at its peak it had over a thousand members and six hundred people in the sanctuary every Sunday. As the congregation grew, so did its need for space. The original Romanesque church on Stainback Avenue was replaced with a neoclassical one behind it on Lischey. Where the old church was heavy and dark, the new one was light and airy. White columns supported a portico that faced Lischey Avenue, and more columns inside supported a balcony around three sides of the large auditorium. A metal awning was erected over the alley between the two buildings so that one could walk from one building to the other without getting wet when it rained. The men of the congregation gathered there on rainy days to smoke between their Sunday school class and the worship service and soon were smoking there every Sunday, rain or shine. The alley became the subject of regular sermons preached on the evils of demon tobacco. The men squirmed in their seats for half an hour several times a year but kept smoking anyway since the Ten Commandments say nothing about smoking and no one had ever heard of the surgeon general.

Next to the two sanctuary buildings on one side was a narrow green lawn fronting Evanston Avenue. On the other side was an enormous parking lot that would have cut through the entire block from Lischey to Stainback, had the congregation not needed one additional building. This was the education building, which was built to the side of the old sanctuary. The education building was a rational three-story structure with a wide corridor down the center of each floor. There were Sunday school classrooms on either side of the corridor, a wide, straight staircase at the end, and one more wide corridor between the new building and the old one. On the top floor was the nursery where Baptists were incubated until old enough to accompany their parents to Big Church. The nursery had a comforting odor of orange juice, saltine crackers and wet diapers. More distinctive than the odors, though, were the sounds. By mounting speakers on the walls of the large room, the congregation ensured that no nursery worker would be without the word of God on Sunday morning. This had the bizarre effect of also ensuring that the members of Grace Baptist Church heard hellfire and damnation preached from infancy. By the time we children were taken to Big Church for the first time, we had heard every Baptist hymn we would ever sing. We had also heard another sound, a strangely soothing sound that came through the speakers once a month just before our parents came to fetch us. The sound could not be compared to any other sound in the experience of a Baptist toddler, though if his father had been a pool shark, the toddler might have likened it to the sound of the break shot that commences a pool game—but with five hundred balls on the table instead of the regulation fifteen.

At age three we received the first of many annual promotions when we were taken one Sunday in September to a Sunday school classroom instead of to the nursery. Sunday school at that age was a simple affair. The teacher would show us pictures of Jesus and tell us how much he loved us and ask if we loved him in return. There were pictures of Jesus holding little children, pictures of Jesus herding little lambs, and pictures of Jesus teaching the multitudes with his disciples close by. We sang "Jesus Loves Me" and "Jesus Loves the Little Children." Some readers may not be familiar with these Protestant classics. The words to "Jesus Loves Me" follow:

> Jesus loves me, this I know,
> For the Bible tells me so.
> Little ones to Him belong,
> They are weak, but He is strong.
> Yes, Jesus loves me. Yes, Jesus loves me.
> Yes, Jesus loves me. The Bible tells me so.

And, while the South of 1959 struggled with the desegregation mandated by the Supreme Court just five years before, in the landmark civil rights case *Brown v. Board of Education*:

> Jesus loves the little children,
> All the children of the world.

THE THOUSAND-PETALED LOTUS

Red and yellow, black and white,
They are precious in His sight,
Jesus loves the little children of the world.

At the end of that first Sunday school class came the biggest moment of our little lives so far. This was the exciting,
terrifying moment when we went to Big Church for the first
time and saw for ourselves the owner of the voice that had
thundered at us through the speakers in the nursery for the
last three years. Our happy parents were waiting out in the
corridor to take us by the hand and lead us through the sunlight
of God's love that bathed the lawn on one side of the building
(and bleached the parking lot on the other) until we reached
the big sanctuary where more of God's love poured through
the tall arched windows.

Unless it was raining, in which case the journey toward
eventual salvation took a very different route through the
labyrinth that had once been the old sanctuary. After the
new sanctuary was completed, the old sanctuary had been
carved into classrooms and choir practice rooms and offices
and storerooms and a dozen other uses for which it was never
intended. It was riddled with twisting staircases and corridors
to nowhere and was nothing like the neat brick ranch houses
we all inhabited in the suburbs. By the time the madman who
had been charged with the project was finished converting
the building into its new uses, the space resembled nothing so
much as the subconscious mind. Indeed, one did sometimes
stumble upon a staircase, a corridor or an entire wing, the
existence of which one previously had never suspected. I once

opened a door to discover a crooked half-stair ascending to a perfectly paneled and perfectly empty windowless chamber that would later become the secret meeting room of the Royal Ambassadors of Christ, about whom more later.

By this time in the journey to Big Church, our fathers had vanished. Bewildered, we children were left clutching our mothers' hands as they picked their way through the maze until at last they reached, at ground level, a narrow low-ceilinged corridor lined with mysterious frosted glass doors. At the end of the corridor was another corridor, so narrow that even children could not walk abreast. It led up—literally up, since the floor was actually a ramp—to an exterior door that deposited the by now completely disoriented children onto an iron staircase that wound upward through a well to the alley above. There we children were greeted once again by our fathers, who beamed at us through the cloud of cigarette smoke in the alley across which we coughed our way for the first time. On the other side of the alley was yet another set of stairs to climb and another corridor to cross until at last, at a pair of wide doors, we accepted the congratulations of an usher and then entered the sanctuary where we would one day profess our faith in Christ before all the world.

My parents sang in the choir. Once my mother had completed the ritual of bringing her child into the house of the Lord for the first time, she handed me over to Mama Fields. I sat on the pew between her and Annelle and watched when they sang the first hymn, my aunt with her florid face, cat-eye glasses and stack of wavy hair, fluting the words in a voice that was not as good as she thought it was, while my prim-faced grandmother carefully sang just below the level of audibility. I took particular comfort in sitting with them because, outside my father, they were the only people in our family who looked like me, that is to say, the only other people with dark, wavy hair—everyone else was blond. I could have been sitting also with Bee Pa and Other Mother, but they never came to church. On Sunday mornings, Bee Pa smoked cigarettes and waited for the ball games that were broadcast on television in the afternoon. Other Mother sat in her rocking chair, reading the newspaper with the help of a magnifying glass. They did not seem worried at all about their prospects for the afterlife, and they could easily be forgiven for expecting that they might ascend to heaven on nothing more than the perfume of Mama Fields's righteousness. My paternal grandmother spent her life in prayer and her mansion in heaven is situated on the town square directly opposite the throne of God. My aunt Annelle is living with her mother in heaven as she did all her life on earth. Whether Mama Fields managed to sneak her husband and her mother-in-law into heaven I will not know until I get there myself.

Mama Fields would purse her lips whenever I asked if Other Mother was going to heaven. I thought this gesture reflected her opinion of ninety-year-old women who powdered their cheeks and wore mascara. Not until many years later did I learn the true reason for her reticence. But before I proceed further with this subject, a short word about my sister, Kim.

There is one talent a person may possess that is almost always unappreciated because, by its very nature, it is almost never displayed: it is the ability to keep a secret. I think most people will agree that the talent is rare. In my sister that talent is coupled with another: the ability to pry secrets out of others. That Kim looked like a little Christian angel when she was a child just made it that much easier for her. When she was still very young, Kim rightly guessed that anybody as holy as Mama Fields must be sitting atop a pile of dirty laundry. I do not know how many years it took her to get it, I do not even know to this day what all was in the pile, but I am fairly certain that however high that pile may have been, Kim is now in possession of all of it. As a child I had little to hide, so it was not until I was well into adulthood that I discovered my sister's twin talents. On the eve of her first or second wedding, my sister opened the vault where she keeps the family secrets and displayed the following treasure, to the amazement and horror of her brothers and first cousin. It goes a long way toward explaining why Mama Fields thought that Other Mother's claim on salvation was dubious at best.

One day Other Mother gave birth to a child whose creation her husband had not only failed to take part in but had failed as well to even notice. The miracle occurred while Other Daddy was at work and was made possible by my great-grandmother's plump figure on which twenty or thirty pounds might easily come and go without comment. Shortly before Other Daddy was to arrive home, Other Mother put the baby in a basket and set it on the doorstep. When Other Daddy burst into the house with God's little blessing in his arms, Other Mother suggested that they adopt the foundling and raise it as their own. Other Daddy agreed. Thus my great-grandmother became perhaps the only woman in history to adopt her own child. Thus too my great-uncle Victor took his place on the family tree, one marked by an asterisk and reached only across a tangle of dashed and dotted lines.

Mama Fields would purse her lips as well whenever I asked if Bee Pa would be going to heaven. That was not the answer I was looking for. I cherished the hope that the whole Fields clan might meet up in the afterlife, as I had always enjoyed their company in this one. My sister called into question the whole notion of a Fields clan when on the eve of one of her weddings she devastated everyone at the table with another jewel taken from her vault of family secrets. This precious gem was the news that not a single person seated there had a drop of Fields blood in them. Evidently Other Daddy had no actual children of his own. Kim had pried out of our grandmother the gold nugget of family secrets, which was that Other Mother had been blessed by God before she married the nominal progenitor of our tribe. Being a gentleman, Other Daddy had given that child the good name that the rest of us have enjoyed ever since. In this he was only following the example of God himself, who from one point of view can be said to have bestowed the same favor on a desperate young girl named Mary.

Seated in a pew for the first time, I naturally looked around first to find my parents. When the choir filed in, Mama Fields pointed them out to me. Not that they were hard to spot. My parents, both twenty-five at the time, were easily the prettiest people wearing robes that day. My mother filed in first, an alto who had to sit in the first row because she was too small to see anything from the second. I took in her honey-blonde hair, the eyes that I knew were green or blue or something in between, and the arch of her brow that suited her playful personality. She smiled and made a tiny wave when she spotted me. My father was taller and sat in the next-to-last row with the baritones. People told me that I favored him because we both had brown eyes and wavy brown hair, though he was much handsomer than I would ever be. He did not wave, but the corners of his eyes crinkled when he spotted me sitting between his mother and sister.

Once I was satisfied that I had not been orphaned that morning, I sat on my knees in the pew and took in my surroundings. On the dais before us were three men in suits sitting on what looked (to three-year-old eyes) like thrones. The associate pastor sat on the left, the minister of music sat on the right, and in the center sat the preacher. Below them in front of the pulpit was a long altar table. Ranged in tiers behind them and wearing maroon robes was the choir. Behind the choir was the most beautiful thing I had ever seen. Set into a tall arched recess in the wall was a baroque decorative flourish that was completely out of keeping with the restrained Protestant interior: a mural depicting the River Jordan as it wound its way from the throne of God in the distance to the baptismal pool that was hidden behind the choir. Throughout my childhood, whenever I was terrified by hellfire or bored with doodling or warned for the last time to stop pestering my sister or else, I would entertain myself by tracing the course of the River Jordan. Just above the baptismal pool itself, the river slowed to a halt in a lush oasis where I would one day be baptized in the name of the Father, the Son and the Holy Ghost amid palm trees and coconuts and other tropical wonders not found anywhere else in Nashville, Tennessee. From there I could follow the bends of the river back through the oasis into a hazy savanna beyond. There, every Sunday, I lost sight of the river as it disappeared around a final bend that led up into a mysterious mountain range. Behind and above those mountains was a glorious cloudbank colored with all the hues of sunrise and shot through with sunbeams. Behind that of course was the throne of God, which the artist had wisely concealed lest the congregation go blind beholding it.

Like every small child, I fussed the first time I learned the source of the mysterious sound that had so enchanted me in the nursery. Once a month, after the sermon, the church had a communion service that Baptists call the Lord's Supper. The fact that communion is celebrated only once a month in a Baptist church is a good indication of how unimportant the sacrament is there, compared to the central place it holds in a Catholic church. It differs from standard communion services in other ways as well. In most Christian denominations, if you want communion, you have to get up and get it. I have joined the lines to receive communion at the altar of all sorts of churches and felt self-conscious in every one of them. In the Southern Baptist Church, a man makes only two trips to the altar (only one if he is gay): one for marriage and one lonely, terrifying trip when he makes a public profession of his faith in Jesus Christ as his personal Lord and Savior. Amazingly enough, nobody ever thought to require that a gay person confess to homosexuality on his or her lone trip to the altar. This explains how so many of us sneak into heaven. More about that later.

In a Southern Baptist church, the body and blood of Christ are served to the seated congregation by the ushers. We might say then that Southern Baptists enjoy communion restaurant-style while the sacrament in other churches may be likened more to a buffet except that no one goes back for seconds. The Lord's Supper begins as the ushers pass chrome platters down each row while the organist plays a special musical selection. On the platters are broken bits of tasteless crackers that the three-year-old naturally grabs for as the platter passes, only to have his little hands gently slapped away by his holy grandmother. Baptists call these crackers unleavened bread; Jews would recognize them as matzos. After every born-again Christian in the room has taken a piece of cracker, the preacher intones Jesus's words from the Gospels: "This is my body. This do in remembrance of me." Then the congregant is free to put the morsel into his mouth. At this time each month, the congregant faces a crucial question: is this crumb so small that I should just let it dissolve, or should I attempt to chew it at the risk of biting my tongue as I chase the little thing around inside my mouth? One would think that a Lord who could feed five thousand with just two fishes and five loaves could also transubstantiate his own body into a platter of full-sized biscuits, particularly since by this time in the service it is well past noon and the Christians are getting hungry.

After serving the body of Christ, the ushers serve his blood. In most churches, the blood of Christ starts off as wine and still tastes like wine, even after it has been turned into Christ's blood through a mystical process called transubstantiation. Baptists do not drink, so this portion of the Lord's Supper consists of shot glasses of grape juice passed down the rows on spill-proof chrome platters. Once again each congregant takes one serving, holds it until the ritual intonement, and then dumps the contents down his throat. The Lord's Supper ends when each born-again Christian sets his shot glass into a round hole bored into a special wooden rack affixed to the back of the pew in front of him. At last,

I knew the source of that sound that had so mystified and soothed me in the nursery.

Unfortunately, the solution to the mystery soon became small consolation for me, as by now I realized that there were no more platters coming and that my grandmother meant it when she said I couldn't have anything served at the Lord's Supper. Every Baptist child hears the explanation every month for years: "Only born-again Christians may partake of the Lord's Supper, and someday when you are old enough to accept Jesus Christ into your heart, you will partake of the Lord's Supper too." In the meantime, nothing. Bad enough that as an adult your only snack in church would be a stingy little crumb and a thimble-full of grape juice once a month, when in the nursery all you had to do was squawk and you got a saltine cracker and a Dixie cup full of orange juice. Even worse was that you would have to wait years to get even that. The final indignity, worst of all, was that your parents—or in my case, Mama Fields and Annelle—would eat right in front of you while you got nothing at all! It therefore should come as no surprise that a sort of quasi–Lord's Supper soon developed in which an adult would slip a peppermint candy or a piece of chewing gum to any child who appeared likely to spin out of control. Still, since some child will always want what it can't have, the solemnity of the Lord's Supper was diluted every month by the fussing and carrying on of one child or another.

Outside of marriage, the Lord's Supper once a month and baptism once a lifetime, the Baptist church has no sacraments. Like other Protestant churches, Southern Baptists stress the importance of a personal relationship with Jesus. That relationship happens through prayer. Baptists are expected to bow their heads and pray in church, before bedtime and before every meal. "Ask the blessing" is what my mother would ask one of her children to do whenever we sat down to eat. My little brother, Miles, fashioned his prayer into a rhythmic formula that began with "Dear God and Jesus" and continued with thanks for our food as well as for the nighttime and the daytime before ending with the standard conclusion to every prayer, "In Jesus's name we pray, amen." Following the blessing would be a typical Southern meal at which there were never fewer than six or seven items on the plate. This would include some sort of meat, dinner rolls or cornbread, a salad or cole slaw, one edible vegetable, and two or three other things that I refused to eat. Every meal ended with a suggestion from my parents that I consider the starving children of India as I decided whether to eat the rest of my vegetables or be sent to my room. Every evening as I trudged off to my room for an hour without television, I imagined an Indian boy my age opening a box my mother had mailed him, full of all the food that I refused to eat. Here is what was in the box:

- Turnip greens
- Spinach
- Asparagus
- Green peas

- Black-eyed peas
- Cauliflower
- Cabbage
- Kidney beans
- Lima beans
- Butter beans
- Three-bean salad
- Beets
- Carrots
- Sweet potatoes
- Fried okra

Was the Indian boy so hungry that he would gladly eat what I had refused to touch? Was it a diet well-balanced enough that he might grow up healthy and strong? Was he a Hindu? Did he know that he was going to hell? And what was he wearing when he opened the box? All I knew about India was how nice Sabu looked in his movies as he flew over Baghdad on his magic carpet, dressed only in a turban and a pair of balloon pants. How disappointed I was when my mother informed me that a flying carpet was not something Santa would bring me for Christmas and that while I was at it, I could scratch the turban and the balloon pants off my list as well.

In those days, I was what we might call "pre-gay." This is, of course, a vague term but has to do with a way of feeling about things that might have met with disapproval had I been foolish enough to introduce it into conversation. For instance, we lived just down the hill from our church's parsonage. Our preacher at the time had three sons, all older than me, all tall and handsome and all with names starting with the letter D. They were the Darby boys: Dwight, Dwayne and Danny. I adored them all. I once stole a rock (see David and Goliath, above) from a shoebox that Danny kept in their garage. I was not a thief by nature but was strangely compelled to put that rock into my pocket and take it home. Also for instance were the flaxen-haired twins down the street who mowed our lawn one summer. Jerry and Terry. Terry and Jerry. The fact that each was powerless to prevent himself from looking just like the other was something that I found strangely moving. Perhaps that was because only a fool would have changed the appearance of either by one molecule.

Also strangely moving for a different reason were the Scaife sisters who would occasionally ride horseback through our subdivision for no discernible reason other than the delight of all who beheld them. LaQuita, LaQuela and LaRawn. They were blonde and beautiful, and I could not help thinking that I could be blond and beautiful as well, if only I would add "La" to my name. One day I did what amounted to the same thing. Overpowered by a sudden desire to express myself, I stole a hat and a pair of high-heeled shoes from my mother's closet, snatched the baby blanket off my brother and fixed it to my waist with a diaper pin, then sailed out the front door in what I imagined at the time to be full drag. How was I to know that my friend Dennis would be loitering at the curb just at that moment? By the time I caught sight of his scalp gleaming in the sunlight through the dark stubble of his hair, he was covering the lower half of his merry face with both hands in a vain attempt to stifle his laughter. What could I do but wobble back inside as fast as I could on three-inch heels and six-year-old legs? The howls of laughter that followed my retreat would nip at the hems of my psychological skirts for years.

A more liberal estimate of the percentage of homosexuals in a given population is approximately 8 percent, or about one in twelve. The implications for Jesus's disciples are immediately apparent. Reading from chapter four of the book of Genesis, where the begats begin, we find that the twelfth male begat upon earth was named Jubal. Verse twenty-one of that chapter says that Jubal "was the father of all such as handle the harp and organ." This suggests that use of the euphemism "musical talent" to denote homosexuality may be as old as homosexuality itself. Of further interest is the fact that the first homosexual was the father of anyone at all. Not only was Jubal the first homosexual, he was also the first gay parent. The Bible does not say whether his children were adopted or whether he begot them in the traditional sense. This is a minor point that need not concern us since, technically speaking, the Savior was not begotten in the usual way either.

We went to church three times a week, on Sunday morning, Sunday night and Wednesday night. Before church on Sunday, we had Sunday school, where we learned all the Bible stories. Before Sunday night service, we had training union, the purpose of which I never understood since we were never trained for anything. On Wednesday night, we had Wednesday night supper, followed by prayer meeting. Children did not go to prayer meeting. The girls went off to participate in GAs, which stood for Girls Auxiliary, while the boys went off to RAs, which stood for Royal Ambassadors of Christ.

The mission of the Royal Ambassadors of Christ was to play touch football in the parking lot, which was itself just a cover for its true mission, which was to give the boys of the church a sanctioned time when they could pick on the sissy in their midst, hereinafter called "me." The RAs were all named David and were all older and bigger than me, except for the new preacher's son, Mark, who was even older and bigger as well as being the handsomest of the bunch with his Roman nose and thick eyebrows. We had a teacher, a bullet-headed young man named Ronnie, whose high school football days were not nearly far enough behind him to suit me. Ronnie was seldom there, but when he was, the RAs would meet in the secret chamber mentioned earlier. There we had some talk about Jesus but a lot more about whatever sport happened to be in season. When Ronnie was absent, the RAs left Jesus behind and played touch football in the parking lot. Once Ronnie found out what was going on behind his back, he started coming more often but only to relive his high school glory days by having us all go out for passes on the pavement. This activity was such a success that Ronnie was inspired to organize a social.

A social is what Christians call it when they get together somewhere other than church to have fun. On a Saturday afternoon, Ronnie and another young man deputized for the purpose drove us out to something that Ronnie swore was a state park but that looked to me like the sort of lonely place where accidents happen to young boys who are remembered ever after for their musical talent. The highlight of the social was a target shoot. Luckily this target shoot happened early enough in the 1960s that all we had to shoot was a BB gun instead of the actual rifles I expect are being fired on such outings today. The prize for winning the competition was a small plastic trophy that Ronnie sat on the hood of his car to inspire us to greatness. We started off with the agreement that we would each fire five rounds, and then a winner would be declared. After all the boys had fired their five rounds, Ronnie invalidated the results with some excuse or other and had us fire five more. At the end of those five rounds, Ronnie once again declared the results invalid and started the contest over. The target shoot ended up lasting all afternoon. After each round, Ronnie identified some new flaw that had crept into the proceedings. Everybody knew what the real flaw was, of course: Mark, who was the star athlete at school and the preacher's son to boot, had yet to hit the bull's-eye. Ronnie was rigging the contest by starting the competition over and over until Mark won a round and could be declared the winner. Everyone understood what was going on, and no one argued with it. We all knew that the longer it took Mark to win, the longer we got to shoot the BB gun. We continued to shoot at the target, and Mark continued to fire wide, until at last we could no longer ignore the fact that it was getting dark.

The setting sun soon left Ronnie with no choice but to hazard the outcome of the competition on the result of a single round fired in what was left of daylight. He announced that each boy would fire one more BB and that whoever got closest to the bull's-eye would take home the trophy. Imagine the surprise of the Royal Ambassadors of Christ when the future homosexual, with his 20/12 vision and hands steadied by years of resisting piano practice, fired a BB right into the center of the target! They all looked so glum. Ronnie's congratulations were so faint. The drive home was so silent. When Ronnie's car finally stopped in my driveway, I leapt out and bolted into the house to share my joy with my parents. The trophy stood on my chest of drawers for years.

Why so glum, Royal Ambassadors of Christ? Could there have been a dawning realization among them that even in the army they might still have to contend with the likes of me? I can only imagine their eventual surprise when they get to heaven and find homosexuals playing for the home team there as well.

These are the things we learned about heaven at Grace Baptist Church:

1. It is not anywhere around here.
2. The streets are made of gold.
3. Everyone lives in a mansion there.
4. We will see all of our dear departed loved ones again when we get there. Grown-ups seemed to get very excited at this prospect. I had never seen a dead person and had nothing at all to look forward to on the dear departed front since all the old people in my family just got older instead of dying.
5. The departed soul loses all interest in his mansion and his loved ones once he follows the sound of angel song to the center of town where God sits in glory with Jesus at his right hand and the Holy Ghost at his left. Baptists have no assigned place for the Virgin Mary but expect to see her seated prominently nearby.
6. The only people who go to heaven are people who have been saved, and the only way a person can be saved is by accepting Jesus Christ as his personal Lord and Savior.

Born again August 15, 1967, Nashville, Tennessee.

Vacation Bible School is a sort of day camp for Baptist children. It lasts one or two weeks in summer and is highly prized by mothers, whose hair is easier to manage without all those kids in it. It takes place at church, of course. Ordinarily it does not differ much from other day camps except for its religious content. But in the summer of 1967, our pastor, Brother Hiram LeMay, a middle-aged version of his handsome son Mark, felt the spirit move him to do an unusual thing. After the processional in which the children marched in to the church to take their seats in the pews and after the singing of "This Is My Father's World" and after we had bowed our heads and prayed God's blessing on another day of Southern Baptist fun, the younger children were marched off to their classrooms while those of us old enough—in Brother LeMay's estimation—to have reached the age of accountability remained in the sanctuary. There the Holy Spirit inspired Brother LeMay to preach a special sermon pitched perfectly to the sensibilities of children aged nine to thirteen. The strategy worked. Sixteen children were snatched from the fires of hell that summer.

Looking back on that summer now, I suspect that there was more to the strategy than just separating out the older kids and preaching to them. Was it just a coincidence that my father chose that week to come into my bedroom one evening and offer to pray with me as I accepted Jesus as my Savior? I doubt it, particularly since no sooner was I saved than he went down the hall and made the same offer to my sister and then to our tow-headed cousin Ricky who was staying over that night. My family accounted for three of the sixteen children who were saved that week, and to my father's mansion in heaven was added a gymnasium and an extra garage. I imagine the heavenly mansions of several other parents got bigger that week as well.

What Brother LeMay figured out under the Holy Spirit's tutelage was that the most difficult part of salvation was not the confession of sins, which is embarrassing enough even for an eleven-year-old, nor the giving of one's life to Jesus, which is terrifying even with the aid of a parent. No, the difficult part of salvation lay in the next step, which is the public acknowledgment of Christ as Savior that is required by the Bible. What the Bible says is "Thou shalt profess thy faith before men." In a Southern Baptist church, provision was made for the public profession of faith at the end of every service when the preacher would step down from the pulpit to the level of mere mortals and invite anyone who had given his or her life to Jesus that week to come down to the altar. For an eleven-year-old boy on an ordinary Sunday, this meant excusing himself past the knees of all the adults in the pew, climbing down the narrow stairs from the balcony where he had forced his grandmother to sit in spite of her arthritis, and stepping up to shake the hand of the beaming pastor before six hundred pairs of eyes all looking to see if his hair was still as he had arranged it that morning, and all of that while trying to ignore the sniggers of the Royal Ambassadors of Christ. Being born again during Vacation Bible School offered the opportunity to rehearse the profession before a small group of kids whose hair was in no better shape than my own and who would be marched together in a pack sixteen strong down to the altar the following Sunday. Even the Royal Ambassadors of Christ recognized that golden opportunity when they saw it and queued up for salvation with the rest of us.

Getting over that hurdle of the public profession of faith meant that each of the sixteen newly minted Christians could now get down to the serious business of figuring out how to prevent our toes from sticking up out of the water when the preacher tipped us over in the baptismal pool. Full-body immersion is what truly separates Baptists from other Christians. In the old days it was done at the riverbank. Most Baptist churches today have special pools installed for the purpose. Baptism is a special service that takes place after the regular worship service on Sunday nights. The new Christian arrives early so that the pastor can show him how to hold his nose in such a way that he won't snort when his upper body is tilted back into the water. Just after the regular service, the pastor goes back to his office where he dons a pair of waders over his suit and then pulls a white robe over that. The baptismal candidate slips into the robing room behind the choir where he puts on a bathing suit brought for the purpose. Worn over the bathing suit is a flowing white robe provided by the church so that a boy will look like an angel when he reaches the bottom of the narrow stairway that leads from the robing room to the baptismal pool. The crucial moment comes when the former sinner wades into the pool. The hem of the white robe spreads out in every direction when it touches the water. Air gets trapped under the robe, which then balloons up around the chest and shoulders. This is the moment of truth. The new Christian must not be distracted by the billowing white robe or the holiness of the occasion, or his toes will fly up out of the water at one end of the pool while his head is being dipped at the other.

That is baptism. As for salvation, I imagine it is something like the experience a groom has just before his wedding. It seems to me that of the many emotions struggling for supremacy in the heart of a young man waiting for his bride at the altar, the chief must surely be abject terror. Not so much fear that he has made a poor choice of life companion, but simple fear of the magnitude of what he is about to do. This is the moment when he does the right thing, the thing that has been expected of him since birth, the thing he has been shaped for and pruned for and directed toward in a thousand subtle ways. All that expectation, both on his own part and on the part of his family and friends and everyone he has ever known, comes down to this single moment, this tiny portal of time through which, by croaking a simple "I do," he must squeeze a whole new way of being into the world. It is the same with the experience of being born again. The Southern Baptist child's whole life has been a preparation for this moment. He is reminded of it at the end of every sermon when the invitational hymn is sung. Every Sunday, the choir invites him to "Come home," "Only trust him," and "Put your hand in the nail-scarred hand." The moment when he realizes that this is it—this is the Sunday, this is the moment when he actually is going to do it—is filled with a wild thumping of the heart inside the chest.

The next emotion I remember from my own conversion experience is one of overwhelming relief. I imagine that my hypothetical groom feels much the same way. Joy comes at the reception, love follows in odd moments during a lifetime with his beloved, but at the moment the knot is tied, the emotion most likely to be felt by the two deer caught in the headlights of expectation is relief. Relief that the suspense is finally over. Relief that one can finally get on with what is to be the rest of one's life. Relief—for any except a Baptist—that one can now finally have a drink. The moment of salvation is every bit the watershed moment in life that marriage is, but the relief is, if anything, more profound. Up to the moment of salvation, the Baptist child's mind has been preoccupied by two things: (1) the list of toys that he wants for Christmas, and (2) fear of eternal damnation in the fires of hell. Salvation does not alter his Christmas list one jot, but it does end, finally and forever, the fear of hell. Finally and forever, that is, if he is a Baptist. Given the life of fear that precedes salvation and the near-fatal palpitations that accompany the moment of salvation itself, it is no wonder that Baptists wisely assert the doctrine "Once saved, always saved." Who would want to go through all that fear again? Baptists preach that salvation is the gift of God and that God is not so petty as to take back what he has freely given. The person who rises from his knees after giving his heart to the Lord embarks on a new life that, however criminal it may later become, is free from the paralyzing fear of hell. In the mind of a boy who has been thundered at from the pulpit for eleven years, that bedrock of fear is dissolved forever. What is left to the boy, then, is the prospect of a lifetime of trying to be more like Jesus. However miserable one's failings at that calling may be, they will not be enough to shut the gates of heaven against him, no matter how long his rap sheet may grow.

Once saved, always saved. A clean break, a new beginning. The boy who gives his heart to Jesus may grow up to be a homosexual, but St. Peter must open the pearly gates for him anyway.

Once saved, always saved. Since even a homosexual can get into heaven, the question once again rises into consciousness: what are homosexuals made of? Boys are made of snips and snails and puppy dog tails. Girls are made of sugar and spice and everything nice. Homosexuals might be made up of some combination of all these things with perhaps a few other ingredients like cashmere and rhinestones sprinkled into the mix. It is also possible that we are made of sterner stuff, since we have a difficult childhood to survive. But whatever the material is, it slips through the pearly gates without setting off the alarms.

Once saved, always saved. The born again homo will stand one day in the presence of the Almighty despite the objections of good Christians everywhere. How can this be? Is the book of life so long that anyone can get his name written into it at no greater price than the gift of his life to Jesus?

In the beginning, God created heaven and earth. And the earth was without form, and void, and darkness was upon the face of the deep. Void. Darkness. Deep. Not much to work with if you've got a world to create, particularly if the kingdom of heaven will be spread out over it. What was God to do? Where to turn for building supplies except to his own omnipotent self? If in the beginning there was God poised to create all created things, it stands to reason that God would have had to use the only material in existence at the time, which was God himself. Now, let us review a few of the things we learned about God at Grace Baptist Church:

1. God exists.
2. God is perfect.
3. God created heaven and earth, and the one is spread out on the other.
4. God is love.
5. God so loved the world that he gave his only begotten son, that whosoever believeth in him shall not perish, but have everlasting life.

If we may safely say that God used the only building material available to him at the time of creation, and if out of that material he created everything that exists, we are led to the following inescapable conclusions about homosexuals:

1. Homosexuals exist.
2. Homosexuals are perfect.
3. Homosexuals are spread out on the earth.
4. Homosexuals are love.
5. Jesus is made of the same stuff as homosexuals.

That homosexuals exist and are spread out on the earth is evident to anyone who is willing to see what is actually in front of him. That homosexuals are love follows logically from our premises, but we prefer to think of ourselves as gay and stop there. That homosexuals derive from God as surely as Jesus does is an indisputable and perhaps inconvenient fact that one cannot wish away if one cherishes the belief—nay, the certainty—that God is the source of all things.

That homosexuals are perfect is an assertion that may puzzle some and outright enrage others. This cannot be helped. I have examined my conscience and found blot after blot there, but I notice as well that each blot is perfect in its inky blackness.

Is it possible that homosexuals are perfect and yet are mistakes as well? If homosexuals are mistakes, are they mistakes on the order of what one might think of as God's greatest mistakes—evil and Satan? Can the creation of homosexuals even be considered apart from the creation of Satan? If homosexuals are perfect, must we regard Satan as perfect also?

The great chain of being assumes degrees of perfection. God at the top, resplendent in the perfection of his perfection. Various choirs below—seraphim, cherubim, thrones, principalities and archangels, all perfect but each somehow less glorious than the choir above, until we descend to the rank of angels, who are willing to roll up their sleeves and take part in the affairs of the world. Then man, who is a piece of work powerful in reason but prone to sin. Next, animals that have to be herded and tamed, weeds that choke the garden, and rocks that are never where you want them. Every lower link in the great chain brings us into greater imperfection until finally, at the atomic level, we find particles that cannot even be depended upon to remain matter or energy long enough to have their picture taken.

In the beginning God created atomic particles, which are notoriously unreliable. In fact, much of what God created cannot even be located but exists as dark matter and dark energy that make up something like ninety percent of the mass of the universe. It seems, then, that if God had truly wished to get rid of all the darkness upon the face of deep, he would have launched a creation lasting at least sixty days instead of only six.

Scientists tell us that supposedly empty space is thickly populated with atomic particles that wink in and out of existence every nanosecond. Thoughts do the same in empty minds. We may think of the universe as the physical body of God, but suppose we think of it as his mind. Suppose those particles with a shelf life of one nanosecond are the half-formed thoughts of God—flashes of inspiration, momentary images of a hamburger when his stomach growls, design ideas for a new homosexual, a new galaxy, a new black hole. God's thoughts are physical realities, but perhaps most of them never make it that far, any more than we could actually make or eat all the hamburgers whose images wink in and out of existence in the mind.

Is the universe, then, God's body or God's mind? Is there actually any difference? If the universe is both body of God and mind of God, can we not simply say that the universe is God and have done with it? Body of God and mind of God. Body of Christ and blood of Christ.

The great chain of being assumes degrees of perfection. But is that really so? Is the Lord's Supper more perfect than orange juice and crackers? More perfect than a hamburger? Is a galaxy more perfect than an atom? A prince more perfect than a frog? Is a heterosexual more perfect than a homosexual? Is a Bible more perfect than any other book, say this one, for example, or a mystery novel if that's what you prefer? Is a dog more perfect than its fleas? Is the universe more perfect than the United States of America, or Somalia? Is heaven more perfect than earth? Is Jesus more perfect than you?

Not long after I was saved, I began to notice in between doodles that Jesus was being crowded out of Brother LeMay's Sunday morning sermons by a new message. This new message had to do with declining church attendance. By 1968, fewer people were making the journey to Lischey Avenue than had done so ten years before. The membership of most mainline Christian denominations actually peaked in the late 1950s. Declining attendance in the 1960s was explained away for a while as a temporary retrenchment in the long march upward toward conversion of every sinner to Christianity and church membership. By 1968, however, even Brother LeMay could not ignore the empty spaces in the pews. Regular attempts to boost attendance failed. Membership declined. At the same time, the neighborhood began to change. At that time in the South, "the neighborhood is changing" was a polite way of saying that Negroes were moving in as white people left their bungalows and narrow lots in town and moved to brick ranch houses on acre plots in the fast-spreading suburbs.

The world was changing fast. My family acquired its first dead person when Bee Pa succumbed to the side effects of his bad habits. His life went up in a cloud of cigarette smoke, leaving Mama Fields, Annelle and Other Mother with no one to drive the bulbous old Plymouth that lay in a coma behind their pink brick house. Something had to be done about finding another driver. Other Mother was ninety-five. Annelle had too many allergies and phobias to drive a car and was afflicted anyway with a condition she called "my inner ear" that caused the room to spin whenever she was asked to do more than drink iced tea or work crossword puzzles or talk on the telephone. Thus, it fell to my grandmother to enter driving school at the age of sixty-five. But first the Plymouth had to be replaced. My father found a used car dealer who would pay a hundred dollars for any car that could be driven onto the lot. On a bright Saturday morning, my brother and I climbed into the backseat of the car for the last time. My father sat in front, and my uncle Raymond, in from Dallas with Aunt Jean, took the wheel. Mama Fields, Annelle and Jean stood at the door to the house and prayed, which was how Raymond got the car started. As we drove over the crest of the last hill leading to the dealership after a terrifying ride through changing neighborhoods in a car that was belching out its life, my uncle Raymond popped the clutch, turned off the engine, and let the carcass roll the rest of the way into the lot. He glided the car to a smooth stop in front of the office and applied the one hundred dollars toward a newer used Plymouth that would end its days, decades later, as a rusted heap in Mama Fields's backyard.

But until the rust and the rot fully set in, the car ferried Mama Fields and Annelle to church every Sunday where as the sixties gave way to the seventies, the sermons gave way from talk of God's love to talk of just who exactly was meant to have it at Grace Baptist Church. The church was in a pickle. The good white folks who made up the congregation were afraid of the new residents of the neighborhood and were especially afraid of leaving their cars unattended for an hour in the church parking lot. They hired a watchman to patrol the lot on Sunday nights. Remembering Christ's injunction to "Go ye unto all the world," it was hard for Grace's remaining members not to notice that the world had in fact come to them. Should they admit black folks into their congregation as the white folks fled, or should the remaining white folks pick up and leave as a body? They needed the black people in the pews to replace the departed white ones. Yet they feared that the presence of black folks in the pews might drive even more white folks away. Would there be enough black folks to pay the light bill for the mammoth church buildings once the neighborhood had changed? And would a congregation more black than white still be Grace Baptist at all?

In the end, no one could do the math. By 1980, Grace Baptist Church had sold its buildings and relocated to a wooded parcel of land far from the center of town and far from any Negroes. Its membership was greatly diminished from its high, twenty years prior. The new sanctuary had none of the stateliness of its predecessor but was what Grace Baptist could afford after selling its land and buildings in the old, changing neighborhood. The church soldiers on to this day, and by the looks of its website, it is a vibrant place to worship the Lord on a Sunday morning. The new members probably know little about the church's glorious past, and its old members are no doubt grateful for the fellowship they still have with each other on a Sunday morning.

My grandmother and my aunt proudly showed me the new church building after it was completed. They continued to go there every Sunday for a while, until at age eighty-five Mama Fields was too old to steer the car over Nashville's hilly roads. She and Annelle discovered a Sunday television broadcast from Woodmont Baptist Church whose pastor they told everyone they liked better than Grace's anyway. The car rusted behind the house, out of sight of the neighbors but in full view of the den where Mama Fields and Annelle huddled around the television set. Mama Fields made notes in the margins of her Bible while Annelle worked the phone, reeling in the news from the congregation at Grace that they would never see again.

My family was long gone from Grace by then. I was nearing thirteen when one Sunday morning my parents announced that we would be visiting another church that day. Five minutes and four blocks later we got out of our Pontiac and walked into Hillhurst Baptist Church. We joined a few weeks later. Maybe we changed churches because my parents, like others, were fleeing the changing neighborhood, or maybe, as I am more inclined to think, they just wanted their kids to go to a church that we could walk to, like they did when they were growing up. My parents did not like Hillhurst as much as they liked their old church. It was new and much smaller than Grace, even its decline. It was relaxed and friendly, but the choir lacked polish and there was no columned balcony and no River Jordan painted behind the baptistery. But the move had its intended effect. Their children flourished at Hillhurst, and for me, at least, the church became, for a couple of years, the focal point of my life.

What I missed most about Grace was the River Jordan. I had spent my childhood trying to follow the course of that river from the lush paradise depicted in the foreground to the clouds and sunbeams in the far distance. The painter of that mural had been none too subtle in suggesting that the Jordan was, in fact, a river of mercy that sprang from the throne of God and flowed from there into the baptismal pool where the miracle of salvation was affirmed. I was never able to make out the source of that river and was never meant to. If the artist knew where God lived, he wasn't telling Grace Baptist Church. All he would tell us was that the center of all things was far away and that its glory was too radiant to behold except as a reflection in the still pool where my sins were washed away.

Of what material does God make a homosexual? How is a gay boy supposed to make a gay man out of the material provided to him by the Southern Baptist Church? Where will the child find God so that he may ask for new supplies, lighter and more flexible materials with which to fashion a man he may become? Where is the center of the universe, where the new equipment is issued?

Hillhurst Baptist Church. A fresh start. No more swimming upstream toward the sunlight of God's love. Would a boy just awakening to his sexual nature find what he needed for that journey by contemplating the simple dove floating above the baptistery in the new church?

I had been born again into the Spirit. I had been baptized into the church. My toes stayed under the water. I was saved. The future homo was on his way to heaven.

PART TWO

JUDGMENT DAY

"Take out the garbage. Mow the yard. Wash the car. Try to be more like Jesus."

Try to be more like Jesus. I heard that a lot when I was growing up. I heard it thundered from the pulpit every Sunday from the time I was old enough to sit still in Big Church without crying or wetting my pants. I heard it in my father's exasperated voice every time I broke something. I heard it when my mother wondered aloud whether some child might be found to take the garbage out before she lost her mind. I did try, too. I tried very hard to be like Jesus.

Hillhurst Baptist was still a new church when my family joined. It had not been there at all when we moved into the brick ranch house in the new subdivision in 1959. The subdivision itself had not been there when I was born in 1956. Hillhurst subdivision sprouted up around a new street called Hillhurst Drive that cut through the fields of what had once been Hillhurst plantation. The old plantation house was still there. The residents of Hillhurst subdivision called it simply "the mansion." Hillhurst mansion was not large by plantation house standards, but it looked plenty big through the eyes of a child. The mansion faced an old four-lane highway called Dickerson Pike. A long weed-choked drive led from the highway to the graceful, columned portico of the big white house. In winter when the leaves were gone, stone outbuildings—slave quarters, we assumed—could be seen off to the left of the house. Hillhurst Drive ran from Dickerson Pike, between a defunct go-cart track to the right and the mansion to the left, down to the neat little ranch houses of the subdivision behind. Looking at the side of the mansion from Hillhurst Drive, one could see a long, single-story wing behind the main portion of the square two-story house. The wing ended in a mysterious stone tower that was three stories high. Hillhurst mansion itself was out of sight of the new houses down the hill behind it, but the stone tower was visible from many parts of the subdivision, our house included.

The mansion was unoccupied and had been for years. It was said to be owned by the former sheriff Robinson. Robinson had not bought such a place on his sheriff's salary. He had bought it with the money he made operating Robinson's Funeral Home on Gallatin Road. It was said that the only thing Robinson used the mansion for was to store coffins. That legend was more effective at keeping out intruders than any fence could have ever been. No one ever went there. From time to time, a strange, unearthly cry would ring out across the neighborhood from the direction of the house. I asked my parents what it was and learned that there was such a thing as a guinea fowl.

I could not understand their explanation of what a guinea fowl was and got it mixed up in my mind with guinea pigs. I imagined enormous shaggy pigs wandering the grounds of the mansion, calling to each other with their piercing, mournful cries. I never saw a giant pig there, but I was amazed one day to see a peacock walking up the hill from an overgrown paddock to the stone tower above.

Rich Acres Drive was the first street in the subdivision that crossed Hillhurst Drive. Our house was on the corner at one end of Rich Acres. Hillhurst Baptist Church was on the corner at the other end, four blocks away. Like the ranch houses around it, Hillhurst had been built to a low-slung modern design. It had no stately white columns or classical interior. The atmosphere was less formal than it was at Grace Baptist, and the dress code was more relaxed. Some among the congregation had a habit of saying "amen" loudly enough to be heard by everyone during sermons. My parents never seemed very comfortable with that, but I quickly got used to it. People were very friendly and no one seemed to mind that their ranks had been infiltrated by a future homosexual.

Or to be more accurate, by a homosexual, period. By the age of thirteen I knew what a queer was and was already going to great lengths to convince myself that I wasn't one. I entertained myself endlessly with fantasies about the life I would lead as an adult. Every version included a wife, lots of children and a big house. There were no other fantasies available to a Baptist boy of that era. In each fantasy, my house was meticulously designed and beautifully furnished. In each fantasy, the birth of twins and triplets and quadruplets went unexplained as year after year the marriage went unconsummated.

One day not long after we joined Hillhurst, the boys of my neighborhood were gathered on my friend Dennis's porch. Someone told a dirty joke, which was nothing unusual, but then Keith, the biggest boy among us, asked a question that I did not quite understand, since it involved an application for the verb "jerk" that I had never heard before. I asked what he meant. Dennis sniggered, made a hand gesture and said, "You do this and think about girls." I quietly said, "Oh." I knew what he was talking about but didn't know there was a name for it. Then the Holy Ghost, who is always hovering nearby, clapped his invisible hands over my mouth before I could blurt out that it worked just as well if you thought about boys.

Anyone looking for sex in these pages will be sorely disappointed. I lost my virginity at the age of twenty, shortly after moving to New York City. Since this is a book about growing up, and since I did not come out of the closet and begin having sex until after I was grown, there will be no sex in this book.

If you bought this book hoping to find repressed Baptist boys fumbling through the joys of first love, I am afraid your hopes will be dashed. I will therefore try to make it up to you by describing all the sex that I was not having.

I will begin with all the sex I was not having with the Boy Scouts of America. One night at the camp my Scout troop attended each year, after all the marshmallows were gone and the fire was low and no one remembered any more ghost stories, I trudged off to the tent I shared with Bruce, the other boy that no one wanted to bunk with and who was therefore my tent mate every year for a week in summer. I peeled down to my underwear, hopped into the sleeping bag rolled out on my cot, said good night to Bruce, and then shot bolt upright when I heard a hello from the other cot, delivered in a voice that did not belong to Bruce and which I immediately recognized as that of a boy named Mark.

I had never trusted Mark and trusted him less than ever that night, since he had set me up for a thrashing earlier that day. I had been walking in the woods between our camp and the next camp over, minding my own business, when I heard the words "There he is!" shouted from the direction of the other camp. I thought nothing of it until two pairs of hands grabbed me under the arms, lifted me into the air, and whirled me around in the direction of the other campsite. Many a gay porn movie has started off with just such an illogical plot device, but at that moment I was too terrified to recognize my potential good fortune. "Give it back!" shouted one of the giants who carried me. "Give it back!" echoed the other. I protested that I had no idea what they were talking about and was still kicking the air uselessly when they brought me to a stop in front of a tent full of boys and said, "We caught the guy who stole your canteen." No lie detector test could have been as convincing as my utter confusion and complete ignorance of any canteen other than my own. When ten minutes of threats produced no change in my story and my protestations of innocence became more and more plainly true, they reluctantly let me go. I was still shaking as I walked back through the woods to my campsite when I heard sniggering coming from the bushes and turned to see Mark emerge from the undergrowth. He was wearing a navy blue T-shirt, just like the one I was wearing. He was also carrying a canteen, even though he was less than twenty yards from camp and in no danger of dehydration. That was when I put it all together—Mark was the same size as me, had wavy brown hair, brown eyes and freckles like mine, and would pass for me if you were a giant from another Scout troop who had never seen the two of us stand shoulder to shoulder.

Now Mark was stretched out in his sleeping bag on Bruce's cot, evidently planning to stay the night. I asked what happened to Bruce, and Mark mumbled some nonsense about variety being the spice of life. You may wonder why I did not jump up and sound the alarm, why I did not evict the changeling and insist that the harmless and genial Bruce be brought back to his own tent where he belonged. Well, the harmless and genial Bruce was not nearly as cute as Mark. I would have been in no greater danger that night had I walked into my tent to find a rattlesnake coiled on Bruce's cot, but my hormones ignored the danger and decided that Mark could stay.

Mark wanted to talk about girls. He went down the list of all the girls at school and slyly asked me what I thought of their looks. I answered all his questions tentatively at first and gradually warmed to the exercise, since it seemed to mean that he actually thought it mattered to me which girl in class was the cutest. I warmed up so much that soon I was jabbering away on the respective charms of this girl versus that one and was even throwing Hollywood sirens into the mix, until at last Mark did not even try to disguise his annoyance when he said, "Is that all you ever talk about?" With that, he yawned, rolled over and went to sleep, leaving me to wonder just exactly what it was that had happened that night.

The next day Mark paid no more attention to me than he ever had except the day before—maybe less. It was not until years later, thinking back on that night, that it occurred to me that a boy who shows up in your tent at night talking about sex might actually be looking for some himself. I had imagined all kinds of evil that Mark might be up to, but the obvious thing never once occurred to me, which was that if a boy wanted to horse around with another boy, he might very well pick the one boy who had no reputation for manliness to put at risk and who might thus be more willing to experiment than another boy. I was so repressed, I could not even imagine the possibility that another boy might make a pass at me.

What I could imagine was a tent full of boys down the hill who had placed bets on Mark's ability to get me into a compromising position that would then be broadcast the next morning from the top of the flagpole so that everyone in Davidson County would know that I was gay. I could imagine that scenario because I had heard something like that before. A friend of mine named Larry once told me about a night he spent in a tent with two of his friends, boys whom I did not know. One, who always slept with his mouth open, fell asleep before the others. Larry inserted the business end of his nether parts into the boy's mouth while the other boy took a Polaroid snapshot of the tableau. Larry had started out that story referring to the sleeping boy as his friend but ended it calling him his slave. He laughed when he said it, and I was never sure whether that meant it was just a joke or if Larry actually used the threat of revealing the photograph to make the boy do things for him. That story was the first inkling I had that just because you like someone, that does not mean you can trust him. I took Larry's story to heart and resolved to repress my sexuality even further, until God had a chance to cure me of it altogether.

Once saved, always saved. Having escaped the jaws of hell, all a Baptist had to worry about for the rest of his life was Judgment Day. Around this time, religious tracts, or we might call them pamphlets, began circulating among the more fervent members of the church. (More on my presence among the fervent shortly.) These pamphlets were wonderful. I could not get enough of them. They were actually tiny comic books, no larger than the notepads on which my mother wrote her grocery lists. Inside each, stories of sin and depravity were drawn in meticulous pen-and-ink miniatures. These were always followed of course by an equally meticulous set of instructions laying out the steps to salvation. The latter part of the pamphlet was of no interest to anyone who was already saved. What was of obsessive interest to a boy of thirteen was the first half of the tract, with its drawings of a licentious life that was forever closed to anyone who had given his life to Jesus. I therefore reasoned that I had better study those pictures carefully since that was all the instruction in the ways of the world I was ever likely to get. And study them I did. I studied them—well, religiously. It was only fitting that these illustrations should play such a big part in my religious education. Illustrations of religious subjects had always been an important part of my upbringing. In fact, at my house they were what put food on the table and clothes on our backs.

Religion has its hierarchies, like all other pursuits. At the top of the Southern Baptist Church is Jesus Christ who is regularly called King of kings and Lord of lords. Below him are arrayed the twelve disciples, with Mary, the mother of Jesus, hovering nearby. The Southern Baptist Church has no saints beyond the Gospel writers to whose names the word "Saint" has been added in the Bible. It does have apostles and patriarchs like Abraham, Moses, David and Paul, and these are ranked alongside or just below the disciples in the religious hierarchy. After them comes Billy Graham, followed by all other evangelists. Baptists may differ in whether missionaries are ranked above or below evangelists, but they will all agree that both rank above regular preachers. After preachers, there is a big falloff in holiness until we reach the ranks of people who are paid to work in the church, like the minister of music or the church secretary. One may also obtain this rank by working for a religious organization like the Baptist Sunday School Board. After all the people who earn their living in one way or another by working for Jesus come the ordinary church members, followed by Easter Sunday Christians, drunkards, thieves, murderers, Hitler and Satan.

My family belonged to a small artisan class of Christians that, like all artisan classes, falls outside the established rankings of society and is therefore suspect while at the same time acknowledged as necessary and even respectable under some circumstances. Nashville is home to the publishing houses of the Southern Baptists and the Methodists, which goes a long way toward explaining why Nashville is the third largest publishing center in the United States. Each year, those houses turn out a steady stream of Sunday school lessons for all ages as well as a torrent of supplementary educational materials. Somebody has to illustrate all that material, and one of the most prolific of those somebodies until his recent retirement was my father.

My father was what he called a commercial artist. He worked freelance. Most of the time he had an office downtown, within walking distance of the Baptist Sunday School Board, but he had a drawing board in the den as well where he would listen to opera while working at home. I was therefore neck deep in religious imagery for much of my childhood. Beyond illustrating, my father sometimes worked as a set designer for religious movies. Mama Fields once babysat Kim and me for two whole weeks while our parents went off to Arizona to make a movie called *Nehemiah*. Though the story concerned the man who rebuilt the walls of Jerusalem, it was a low-budget movie to say the least, which meant that everyone involved was offered the chance to appear on camera as long as they would do it for free. I will never forget my pride at seeing my turbaned father peer over the half-built wall of Jerusalem to shout, "Throw me a hammer!" in his Southern accent, nor my anxiety when my mother, her blonde hair covered by a veil, was scooped up and carried off-camera by a heathen horseman.

My father worked occasionally on outdoor religious plays as well. I vividly remember one such spectacle based on the life of Moses. The scene when Moses yanks two stone tablets out of the side of a plywood mountain while lightning flashes all around was particularly thrilling to a young Christian. When the play closed, our Pontiac was moved into the driveway to make room in the garage for a golden calf that my father had made for the show and didn't know what to do with afterward. We kids loved that golden calf. It was great for playing cowboys and Indians on a rainy afternoon, and soon all the kids in the neighborhood were clambering over it. This made my mother nervous. She was apprehensive lest someone at church find out that we had a pagan idol in our garage. She began to remark whenever my father was in earshot that Moses had found a way to get rid of his golden calf and that if my father put his mind to it he could get rid of ours, too. The Pontiac was soon back in the garage. My prayers for a production of Jonah and the whale went unanswered.

My favorite religious pamphlet was the one that described the Apocalypse—favorite, that is, until I got to the end where Judgment Day was drawn in minute detail. Up to that point, it was just titillating pictures of the Four Horsemen skewering fornicators on the ends of their pikes, and Jesus in glory floating down into the orgy that was still going on among the sinners who hadn't drowned in the river of blood. In the picture of Judgment Day, a huge crowd was seated in a celestial amphitheater. On the stage surrounded by angels were God, whose features were difficult to make out in the midst of his radiance, the Holy Ghost, who had no features at all, and Jesus, easily recognizable as he smiled and waved to the crowd. Behind them on the stage was a giant movie screen. Playing on the screen was a movie that God, Jesus and the Holy Ghost had spliced together. The movie showed every sin ever committed by every person who had ever lived. There was no popcorn, no getting up to go to the restroom. Instead, the crowd sat in queasy silence, waiting for the moment, eons away on this eternal day, when their own foibles would be projected in galactic scale for all creation to see.

As I studied the picture of Judgment Day, I began to cast about in my mind for ways that I could turn this scene to my advantage or at least emerge with my eternal reputation intact. I thought of my mother's little bird and how bored it must have been reporting the trivial misdemeanors of a Southern Baptist child. I thought of my straight-A report cards stretching back for years and of the J. S. Bach two-part invention I was learning to play. I thought about Ewing Park Junior High School and my exalted positions there on the honor roll and the student council and the Cougar Patrol. I played out in my head a movie of my own making. In it were all my adventures in Sunday school and training union. There were warm evenings of fellowship with the Royal Ambassadors of Christ gathered around the piano. There were heartwarming moments of "Please" and "Thank you" and "You're welcome" and "Beg your pardon?" There were moments of comic relief when my mother would glare at me until I yielded my seat to an old person or held a door open for a lady. There was romance as well, not a subplot exactly since there was no action and therefore no story, just the chaste love affair with Janet Davis, a pretty girl with a round face and pale hair who held a place on the honor roll close to my own. I had managed to keep my toes underwater during baptism, and that scene was played to great effect as well. All in all, I thought that if the movie shown by the Holy Trinity bore any resemblance to the one I was cobbling together in my head, Judgment Day might not be so bad after all.

Then I turned the page and my heart froze. There, emblazoned across the top of the page in colossal letters, were the words "Even your thoughts will be revealed!" The movie projector in my head stopped turning, the house lights went up, and I panicked. A different and far more interesting movie was now threaded into the projector. My mental theater was darkened once again and the new movie began to play. My cheeks burned and icy hands of fear closed around my throat as I watched that movie and realized the inescapable truth: it was smut! Actually, not just smut. The movie had interludes of another genre that I did not recognize at the time but would later learn is called a snuff film. But mostly it was just smut, and though I tried to splice in some smut that was at least regulation heterosexual smut, the projector was spinning too fast, was spinning out of control in fact, lights projecting frame after frame, reel after reel of male single-sex porn. I would still get into heaven—I was a Baptist, after all—but I would never be able to hold my head up and join in the celestial chorus of praise gathered around the Almighty. It was unlikely that I would even be able to take my place in the modest but pleasant suburbs at the edge of town. No, I would be living in a pup tent in the woods surrounding heaven, permitted to come into town only on market days and then only long enough to be hooted at before I slunk away in shame.

Thus began my prayer campaign to Jesus for the miracle that would change Pinocchio into a real boy. I had prayed for that miracle before, of course, but never so earnestly as I did now. I wanted to be like the other boys. Homosexuality at that time was still the sin that dared not speak its name and so was rarely mentioned, beyond the occasional "sissy" that I heard whispered as I walked down the halls at school in my Cougar Patrol sash. The bullies were circling but dared not say anything out loud or lay a finger on me. They knew perfectly well that the faculty and the administration were looking out for the reigning champion of the honor roll.

It also helped that the other members of the Cougar Patrol were not only the star athletes of the Ewing Park Cougars but held places on the student council and the honor roll themselves. My relationship with them was complicated, but it was generally understood that an elite needs artists and intellectuals among its number. In the social pecking order, I therefore was assigned a position on the fringes of the ruling class. I was easily the most visible future homosexual at school, but my fame protected me instead of making me a target. I was safe but isolated, respected but reviled. What child in that position would not pray nightly to Jesus for the miracle that would change him into a normal boy like everyone else? After all, the Bible promises us that all things are possible in Jesus. Sunday after Sunday, thundered from the pulpit were heartwarming stories of murderers and drunks who were snatched from the jaws of hell by the redeeming power of the Lamb of God. At times it seemed a wonder they could keep the prisons full and the taverns open what with all the sinners leaping into the Everlasting Arms. There were no stories of reformed harlots or drug addicts or homosexuals since such things belonged to a demimonde too perverse to be mentioned in a church. But the implication was clear. If Jesus can make an honest man out of a lying, thieving, murdering drunkard, he can make a straight boy out of you. All things are possible with Jesus. I knew that if I died tomorrow, the movie of my thoughts that would be shown on Judgment Day would scald my soul. But if Jesus would turn me into a heterosexual, the movie at least would have a happy ending. I redoubled my prayers. I prayed nightly, daily, hourly for Jesus to change me into a real boy.

Then there was all the sex I was not having with my friends. We talked about it, mostly in the form of dirty jokes that I listened to and laughed at but never told myself, lest Jesus add the footage to the movie that would be shown on Judgment Day. All those dirty jokes my friends told put us in an awkward position with respect to our fathers.

We all knew that our fathers were supposed to talk to us about the birds and the bees. It was hard to imagine that a father could have anything to add to what we had already learned in the schoolyard. If mine did, I figured there were only two possible ways he could do it, neither of which appealed to me. The first was that my father would feel compelled to describe sex in even more detail than in the hundreds of dirty jokes

I had heard, which would be embarrassing. The second was that my father would want to teach me all the science behind sex, which would be redundant because I had already looked it up in the "S" volume of the *World Book Encyclopedia* that my parents bought from a door-to-door salesman. But what I dreaded more than anything my father might say was what my father might ask. If he was going to ask me about my own interest in girls, and what would be even worse, about my experience with them, then I was going to pray God to take me into his bosom right then and let me skip the rest of a life too embarrassing to endure into old age. I was therefore relieved beyond measure when one evening upon his return from work, my father dropped a sheaf of booklets on my dresser and sheepishly muttered, "Take a look at those." That was the whole of my official sex education.

Dad had obviously picked up the booklets at the Baptist Bookstore, which was just around the corner from the Baptist Sunday School Board where he went every week to drop off his finished illustrations. As I leafed through the booklets, I was amazed that the Sunday School Board had been able to find a Baptist author who would write so frankly about sex. He even wrote about homosexuality. I knew what he would write, but I was deeply saddened anyway when I read that a boy who finds himself with homosexual longings faces an uphill battle and a difficult life. Part of what would make it so difficult is that he would not have much time for fun after all the praying he would need to do to compel God to cure him of his homosexual desires. Well, I already knew that. I heaved a sigh and read on. The author was careful to let his readers know that all the adults out there were aware that many boys would experiment sexually with each other before going on to a lifetime of marriage, parenthood and Christian service. "Just horsing around" was what I had heard such experiments called. I dreaded it as much as I dreaded a talk about the birds and the bees. I dreaded it right up to the moment one night in the attic his parents had converted into a bedroom when my friend Mike proposed that we horse around, by which he meant that we horse around with our own horses but in unison. I blushed a hundred shades of scarlet and refused.

Mike persisted. "I can't ask Burt because Burt would tell," he said. That seemed like spurious logic to me. Who was Burt going to tell? His parents? The other kids at church? Was he going to step to the microphone at the next school pep rally and say, "Excuse me, I have an announcement to make"? Burt would not tell any more than I would, any more than Mike would. I did not refuse because I was afraid Mike would tell. I refused because I was afraid of what Mike himself would think of me. I refused because I was afraid that I would do something or say something that would make it clear that I was far more interested in horses than Mike was. I was afraid, in other words, that he would think—or more accurately, that he would discover—that I was gay.

Mike never brought up the subject again. He thought I was a prude for refusing to horse around, but that was okay with me. We were Southern Baptists. We were supposed to be prudes.

What is the old joke about Southern Baptists?

"Why do Southern Baptists condemn sex before marriage?"

"Because they're afraid it will lead to dancing."

And then there was all the sex I was not having with the boys at school. The only boys at school who actually wanted to know me were the other geeks on the honor roll. I was therefore dumbfounded when one summer night I answered the doorbell to find a big shambling boy named Ricky standing under the moths circling the porch light. Ricky had a pronounced drawl and seemed like a boy who still had a lot of relatives living in the country. I only saw him wear socks in winter, and it never occurred to me then that maybe his family could not afford socks year round. I had known Ricky since third grade, but we had never been friends and seemed less likely to become friends with each passing year. I had never sought his company at school and he had never sought mine, yet here he was, miles from home, standing on my doorstep, awkwardly trying to crank up a conversation. I was so stunned by the sight of him that I did not even think to invite him in, nor did I join him outside. I just hovered in the doorway and marveled that this bashful boy wanted to be my friend, in spite of the fact that we were miles apart socially at school and miles apart physically at home.

Two weeks later, I looked up from a book I was reading out on the lawn and saw a boy named Darryl walking up Rich

Acres Drive. Darryl was a funny boy with a mournful face who lived with his grandparents in an old house that had once stood on a hill but, thanks to a passing tornado, as he told it one day in science class, was now situated in the valley below. Darryl lived even farther away than Ricky and, while not as evidently poor, his clothing suggested that he had at least one older brother upon whom that clothing had looked fresher than it did on him. Like Ricky, Darryl had never sought my company at school and yet had walked for miles just to pay me a call and maybe strike up a friendship. I was out of high school before it occurred to me that both those boys may have set out from home for another reason, that they might have had a dim notion that friendship with an effeminate boy like me might offer opportunities beyond mere companionship. It was not until years later, in other words, that it occurred to me that both those boys might have actually come a-courtin', or at least looking for someone with whom to horse around.

Neither Ricky nor Darryl returned, and I did not seek them out at school. Had either of them shown up on my doorstep with flowers, or written me a love note, or grabbed me under the bleachers and kissed me, things might have been different. Not that showing up with flowers would change the fact that you are reading a book that has no sex in it. You might think that I fervently wished for a world in which one of those boys might show up at my door with a bouquet of flowers, a world in which I might kiss a boy and hold hands with a boy and some day round all the bases with a boy that I loved. I did not. Such a world was unimaginable to me, and I had a vivid imagination. I might lust for a boy, I might even have a crush on one, but I never felt any longing for a world in which that would be normal and acceptable. I did not long for a world in which I would be accepted for what I was. In order to do that, I first would have had to accept *myself* for what I was. I could not bring myself to do that. Instead, I prayed continually, prayed without ceasing, that one day I would not be a homosexual. And until that day came, I refused to admit or accept that what I was, was what I would always be. My prayers to God were that I might be changed so that I fit into the world. I never once asked that the world might change to make room for me.

What are homosexuals made of? If, when the universe was made, there was no material available to God other than God himself, we are cornered into admitting that everything that exists was made from one perfect material. What are homosexuals made of? God himself, of course, just as surely as any quark that has winked into existence for the merest nanosecond is nothing other than full glory of God. Just as surely as Jesus Christ himself was and is, in whatever form or lack thereof, made up of God himself. The rules of logic forbid me at this juncture to assert that Jesus was therefore a homosexual. There are legions of us who would like nothing better than to recruit Jesus Christ into the ranks of famous homosexuals of history. The fact is, though, that the evidence for such a claim is as scant as it is for just about every other assertion that Christians have made about our Lord for twenty centuries.

What do we really know about Jesus? Plenty of ink has been spilled in the search for the historical Jesus over the last century. The search has not been a waste of time at all since new Gospels are discovered all the time, stuffed into crockery all over the ancient world. In Egypt, in particular, it seems a person cannot reach into an old pot without pulling out a Gospel. The Gospel of Thomas is the most famous of these twentieth-century discoveries, but there are many others. Most of them are just fragments, and very few add even one jot to what we know about Jesus of Nazareth.

What sort of person was Jesus? What sort of human being? Leave aside for the moment the advantages of his divine paternity. After all, my own parents, who are still living and in decent health, are as truly divine as either parent of Jesus. How could it be otherwise, if the only substance that exists is God?

The sons of Rockefellers and Vanderbilts are flesh and blood just as surely as are the progeny of Hatfields and McCoys. They are the same substance, however great the distance between their social ranks. You are the child of God, however dubious your lineage, just as surely as Jesus was. You are the same substance, made up of the one perfect God. That Jesus was begotten directly of God does not make Jesus more perfect than you. Your ancestors may have slithered along lake bottoms for eons before they could evolve into you, yet the ancestors and the slithering and the lake bottom—and you—have never been less than perfect. There are no degrees of perfection. If something is perfect, it is *perfect*, regardless of the time and distance that separates it from its source. The child sired directly by God himself can only be more perfect than Mr. Hatfield's son if the Hatfield was somehow a mistake. Otherwise, we must admit that perfection begat perfection down through the eons until Mr. Hatfield's ancestor begat a creature with a perfect set of lungs and so on, down to the day when Mr. Hatfield's perfect son, in a perfect rage, took aim at the perfect McCoy across the hollow.

Leaving aside the question of Jesus's paternity, then, let us ask what sort of person he was. We will start with what facts we have. Here is what the best modern scholarship can tell us, to a reasonable degree of certainty, about the man called Jesus.

Jesus was born around the year 5 BCE, when Herod was king in Judaea. He was most likely born in Nazareth, a town in Galilee that was a region of Judaea that was itself a troublesome backwater of the Roman Empire. His parents were named Mary and Joseph. He had several sisters and brothers, one of whom, James, went on to become head of the Christian church in Jerusalem. Jesus was baptized in the Jordan River by John the Baptist and was most likely a follower of John for a time. Jesus's own followers were both male and female, and it is likely that some of Jesus's early followers were originally followers of John. After John's arrest, and after a possible vision quest, Jesus returned to Galilee. There, he began a career as a miracle worker, a profession that was evidently more common in his day than it is in ours. He walked from town to town casting out demons and healing the sick. He also taught. What he taught was something that he called the kingdom of heaven. The good news he proclaimed is that the kingdom of heaven can be found right here, right now, on earth.

Jesus's relations with other people were not always harmonious. When he showed up to teach in his hometown, his family evidently thought he had lost his mind and tried unsuccessfully to get him off the streets and out of sight. The Pharisees, a religious sect of the time, were distressed by Jesus's relaxed attitude toward the Jewish laws governing purity and observance of the Sabbath. They were irked as well by Jesus's refusal to demonstrate his abilities by working wonders for them.

No one knows what offense led to Jesus's Crucifixion at the order of Pontius Pilate, the Roman governor of Judaea. Jesus was just one of many who were crucified by the Romans. Jesus's death occurred around the year 30 CE.

And that's it. Everything else is conjecture, confabulation, fantasy, or misprint. Jesus was not considered important in his time. He did not become important until after his death. It would be thirty years before anyone would think to sit down and write out a story of Jesus's life. By then, that is just what it was—a story. The people who actually knew Jesus had joined him in heaven by then. Imagine how your own life would read if it were fashioned thirty or more years from now out of the gossip that was still available to a biographer who never knew you. Consider, for example, my own account in these pages of events that occurred in the life of my own great-grandmother, stories arising from a time before my birth about a woman I actually did know and that yet may or may not be true.

The past does not exist. What exists are memories, and memories are thoughts. God's thoughts arise out of the cosmic void like lotus blossoms in a pond and are shaped into a pattern we call creation. Our thoughts arise from the void and are shaped into patterns as well. The architect arranges thoughts into blueprints, the musician into music, the chef into recipes, the scientist into theories. You arrange thoughts into a picture you would like to present to the world each morning when you get dressed. The novelist arranges thoughts into novels and the historian into histories. Matthew, Mark, Luke and John arranged them into Gospels. The gospel truth.

Now let us compare the bare-bones life of Jesus set forth above to the more colorful story told in the Gospels. After all, it is the Jesus of the Gospels whom the young Christian is told to emulate. Here is what the Gospels tell us about Jesus:

1. Jesus was special from the moment of his birth. Angels sang and kings brought gifts. Shepherds brought their sheep. Christmas carols further elaborate this scene by describing the calm of the stabled animals, who instinctively knew that this was the son of the same God who directed the first man to give them their names.

2. Being the only begotten Son of God conferred certain advantages, like being perfect from the get-go. The first story of Jesus's perfection starts off looking like a mischievous prank. Jesus's mother, Mary, and his earthly father, Joseph, were halfway home from a visit to Jerusalem when they noticed that twelve-year-old Jesus had given them the slip. They rushed back to Jerusalem, ready to give him a piece of their mind, only to find Jesus lecturing the elders in the temple. The elders were amazed at the boy's understanding of the Scriptures. His parents gave him a piece of their mind anyway, just like my own parents, who never failed to call me "Mr. Smarty-Pants" whenever I attempted to emulate Jesus by lecturing my elders.

3. There are no stories at all about Jesus between the ages of twelve and thirty. I hope that outside of what I set

forth in these pages, the same will be true for me. Is it possible that the only begotten also believed that the less said of his youth, the better?

4. It is probably safe to say that Jesus's toes stayed under the water when he was baptized since immediately afterward, the heavens opened up, a dove descended on a sunbeam, and a deep voice from heaven said, "This is my beloved son, in whom I am well pleased." As a child, I would close my eyes and try to vanish whenever my parents called that much attention to me. Jesus did indeed vanish shortly after his baptism by wandering off into the desert for forty days and nights. There was nothing in the desert to eat and nothing to do but pray. In Native American traditions, this kind of spiritual exile is called a vision quest. Spiritual retreat is a feature of all religions. Some would argue that it is an essential feature for any spiritual seeker who sets foot on the road to enlightenment. What visions Jesus may have had are not recorded. What is reported in the Gospels are three visits from Satan, who tempted Jesus to take advantage of his heavenly birthright by performing miracles so dazzling that mere mortals would rush to crown him their king. Jesus refused and never spoke to Satan directly again.

5. Jesus's first miracle was at the marriage feast in Cana, where he turned water into wine. This chapter of Jesus's life makes Southern Baptists nervous, though few will ever admit it. Baptists don't drink. Mama Fields, one of

the great Southern cooks, would not even allow cooking sherry in her kitchen. My mother forgot herself one Christmas and tried out a new dessert recipe called bourbon balls. My sister and I looked everywhere for the bottle that the bourbon came in but never found it, which leads me to believe that the entire contents of the bottle were emptied into the bourbon balls. Annelle had never tasted anything like them. As the afternoon wore on, she praised my mother's cooking more and more until by 4:00 she was so drunk with admiration she could hardly stand. The next year there were no bourbon balls at Christmas. Baptists have never really understood how the Savior could call himself a Baptist and yet provide the wedding guests of Cana with yet more wine, when they had clearly had enough to drink already. Baptists would much prefer that Jesus had left the water just as it was. They would be even happier if Jesus had turned all the wine in Cana into iced tea as soon as he got to town.

6. Jesus apparently had a handful of disciples when he showed up in Cana. After he left, he called the rest. He is reported to have done so by simply saying to the prospective disciple, "Follow me." That's all it took. I suspect that recruiting followers was a simple matter for someone who had a reputation for turning water into wine. In fact, there is every reason to believe that Jesus was the life of the party. Luke has Jesus say that although John the Baptist was an ascetic, Jesus himself

"came eating and drinking." Baptists know that passage perfectly well and yet you will never hear it preached in a Baptist church. One might imagine Jesus and his merry band of twelve attracting a lot of attention as they wandered from town to town. Thirteen young men coming into town could be expected to arouse the interest of at least thirteen young women, the jealousy of their thirteen boyfriends, and the suspicion of their thirteen fathers. Mathematics has never been my strong suit, but using even the shakiest of calculations, it is easy to see how thirteen young men could attract a mob of five thousand by mid-afternoon, especially when one of them could turn the Sea of Galilee into a giant punchbowl with a snap of his fingers.

7. Once Jesus had his disciples in place, the miracles began in earnest. The Gospels are, for long stretches, a shaggy-dog story in which Jesus goes from one town to the next, casting out demons, healing the sick, and dumbfounding the Pharisees with his wisdom—with his wit as well, if he was indeed the life of the party, as I've suggested. Sprinkled in among the workaday miracles are stories of truly staggering wonders like walking on water and raising the dead. Jesus was also one of the great raconteurs of history, and the Gospels are enlivened throughout by the stories he told wherever he went. Throw in the oddly compelling human-interest story, like the one about the Samaritan woman at the well or the young man who was afraid to give up his fortune

to follow Jesus, and it is easy to see how generation after generation of Christians has been transfixed by the Gospels. Jesus set a high standard for his followers, which has not stopped legions of Christians from trying to measure up to it. Indeed, I suspect that if Sears & Roebuck had offered a Jesus costume in its catalog, I would have spent my childhood trying to walk on water instead of jumping off the picnic table in a red cape.

8. Jerusalem was to Jesus what the flame is to the moth. Perhaps it was the memory of his early success there as a preteen lecturer that drew him to return. Like many a young man before and since, he was drawn to the big city, but his visits as an adult did not garner the rave reviews he received as a child. One of the all-too-few pictures in my childhood Bible was of Jesus driving the moneylenders out of the Temple with a scourge that I asked to have for Christmas every year but never got. Around this time, Jesus added prophet to the list of his occupations as he began to predict the eventual destruction of the Temple. Christians today think of these adventures in Jerusalem as yet more examples of Jesus's holiness. Not everyone at the time would have seen it that way. If we stop to remember that the man who predicted the destruction of the Temple was followed everywhere by a mob, it is easy to see that the authorities in Jerusalem might have regarded Jesus in somewhat the same light as the United States government regards terrorists. Estimate, if you will, the life expectancy of an

Osama bin Laden were he to ride down Pennsylvania Avenue on a donkey while his admirers sing hosanna and lay palm branches in his path. Remember that there was no constitutional right to assembly or to free speech in those days. Remember, too, that the authorities had no idea that Jesus was the Son of God. Today, we think that it must have been obvious to anybody after the eighth or ninth miracle that Jesus was no ordinary mortal. What the Bible does not tell us, but historians generally agree upon, is that wonder workers were rather thick on the ground in those days. We might take a charitable—in fact, Christian—attitude toward the people who killed our Lord if we consider that it may have been difficult for them to tell one wonder worker from the next. We might therefore forgive them for being indifferent toward the entire subject of wonder workers when the real deal came along. Modern Christians may criticize the Jewish Temple elite and the Roman governor for not believing Jesus when he plainly stated that he was the Son of God. However, a close reading of the Gospels reveals that Jesus himself never claimed to be the Son of God in their presence. In fact, only once in the first three Gospels does Jesus identify himself as the Son of God. In those three Gospels, called the synoptic Gospels, Jesus often refers to God as his father, but so do you and I whenever we recite the Lord's Prayer. What Jesus called himself in the synoptic Gospels—and over a dozen times as well in the Gospel of John—was the son of man. "Son of man" was a phrase that was roughly equivalent to the modern "son of a gun"—yet further evidence that Jesus was a lighthearted soul who knew how to spin a good yarn and have a good time.

9. It is difficult to gauge the status of Jesus at his death. On the one hand, he was sold for thirty pieces of silver, traded by the mob for a ruffian named Barabbas, and crucified on the hill of skulls between two thieves, one of whom you will meet when you get to heaven. On the other hand, if Jesus was worth no more than that, why were both the Roman and the Jewish authorities so reluctant to take responsibility for his execution? Was it that once they came face-to-face with him, they had some inkling that here was something beyond any wonder worker they had ever seen?

10. In the Gospels of Matthew, Mark, and Luke, Jesus admits only once to being the Son of God and only twice to being the Christ. In the Gospel of John, he talks of little else, to the point where one cannot help but be reminded of the line from *Hamlet* where Gertrude says, "The lady doth protest too much, methinks." On the other hand, the synoptic Gospels record sixty-six instances in which Jesus refers to himself as the Son of Man. The implication is clear. Christ, Messiah, Son of God—those titles were added to Jesus's legend after his death by writers who could not otherwise understand how one man could have such an impact on so many people. The titles call to mind a popular

story told about Siddhartha Gautama, a man more widely known as the Buddha. After his enlightenment, Siddhartha wandered across India, teaching what he called the Middle Way. He collected followers, just as Jesus did. Other than carrying a begging bowl, he traveled empty-handed, as Jesus advised his followers to do. Perhaps it was because the Roman Empire did not rule India that Siddhartha was able to live in this manner to the ripe old age of eighty. The story goes that when Siddhartha came to a town, the people there, marveling at his teachings, would ask him what sort of person he was. "Are you a god?" they would ask, and Siddhartha would answer no. "Are you a king, then?" they would ask, and he would once again answer no. "Well, if you are not a god and not a king," they would ask, "what are you then?" Siddhartha's simple answer was, "I am awake." It was not long before Siddhartha Gautama came to be known simply as the Buddha, which means "awakened one." People needed a title for the extraordinary Siddhartha, and so they called him Buddha. People need a title for the extraordinary Jesus, and so we call him all manner of things that he never called himself.

11. The Buddha taught awakening. Jesus taught something he called the kingdom of heaven. He said that it "is spread out on the earth, and men see it not." Is this the reason both Romans and Jews were so reluctant to kill him? Did they, ever so dimly, see a glimpse of heaven reflected in the eyes of Jesus of Nazareth, the

Son of Man, when he was brought before them for judgment?

12. Something happened shortly after the Crucifixion of Jesus that changed the world forever. Baptists, like other Christians, believe that Jesus rose bodily from the dead after three days in the tomb and that he spent forty days with his followers before his ascension into heaven. I am unwilling to rule out the possibility that these things—or something like them—occurred. There are stories of similar feats performed by the yogis of India. One of those yogis, Patanjali, gave instructions on how to perform most of the miracles of Jesus in a short book published under the title *How to Know God*. The book can be found in any large bookstore, but we will no more be able to recreate Jesus's miracles by following Patanjali's instructions than I was able to re-create my great-grandmother's biscuits by following her recipe. I was once part of a gathering where an imam described seeing a Sufi master slice open his own belly with a knife and then instantly close it by running his thumb over the incision. "I saw it with these eyes," the imam said, and I can think of no reason why he would lie about such a thing. I myself once saw a psychic perform one of the miracles of Jesus, called a transfiguration, in which a spirit superimposed his features over hers so that she appeared to have a long, bearded face. Rather than discount entirely the miracle upon which the world's dominant religion is based, I prefer to heed, with Horatio, Hamlet's admonition that there are more

things in heaven and earth that are dreamed of in our philosophies.

13. The most intriguing explanation for the Resurrection of Jesus comes from a tradition known as esoteric Christianity. Esoteric Christianity is a school of thought that regards Christianity as a mystery religion. It traces its roots back to what it asserts are secret teachings that Jesus gave to the twelve disciples. The Bible alludes to secret teachings several times, when a particular Gospel story ends by saying that Jesus took the twelve aside and taught them separately. Jesus himself later changed the name of one of those disciples to "the Rock"; that leads me to wonder whether the twelve required additional teaching because they were unusually thick-headed. The esoteric tradition, however, holds that in these private sessions, Jesus passed on arcane teachings, including something now known as the resurrection body. There are similar teachings in other religions. Taoists speak of a diamond body, Sufis of the most sacred body, and Tibetan Buddhists of a rainbow body. Reading between the lines of biblical scriptures, ancient practitioners of esoteric Christianity discerned that the resurrection body will have several highly desirable properties. Among them are:

    1. immortality
    2. physical beauty
    3. an inner glow
    4. freedom from pain

5. freedom from gravity
6. the ability to pass through objects without harming them
7. genitalia (!)

The best news of all is that every Christian will get one of these resurrection bodies at the Second Coming of Christ, just in time for Judgment Day. I, for one, will gratefully exchange this mortal coil for a resurrection body when the time comes, and I hope to meet all my readers in your perfected forms as well.

14. "Light body" is the term most often employed by spiritual seekers today to describe the perfected and immortal form of the physical body. "Light work" is a term used to describe spiritual practices that lead to the conscious creation of the light body. Light workers believe that they need not wait until the Second Coming to receive a light body but that it can be created now. This belief is not something that was plucked recently out of the thin atmosphere of the New Age; it is an ancient esoteric tradition, the murky origins of which date to well before the time of Jesus. Esoteric Christianity explains the Resurrection by simply asserting that Jesus had his light body in place and ready to go before his arrest. The theory handily explains the miracles attributed to Jesus after his Resurrection. Those last miracles were of a different order than the miracles assigned to the years of Jesus's ministry. In the days following his Resurrection,

Jesus's miracles have some of the quality of comic book superpowers. There were no more exorcisms. There were no more healings. After his Resurrection, Jesus walked through walls. He glowed in the dark. He faded in and out of view like the Invisible Girl. In the Ascension itself, he levitated up into a cloud. Consider the story of Thomas, who famously doubted that the Jesus standing before him was the same Jesus he'd followed before the Crucifixion. His doubts are understandable. The Gospels record that the first people who encountered the resurrected Jesus did not recognize him. Jesus offered to prove his identity by showing Thomas the wound inflicted by a Roman sword during his Crucifixion. He even invited Thomas to thrust his hand into the opening. Thomas declined the invitation at the last second, dropping to his knees instead to worship the risen Lord and thus sparing generations of Christians the horror of reading what surely would have been one of the most grisly episodes in the history of religion, *if*—that is, *if*—Jesus had been present in his revivified thirty-three-year-old physical body. The theory of the resurrected light body makes much more sense in the context of this story. In his light body, Jesus could extend his invitation in confidence, knowing perfectly well that Thomas would not only be able to fit his hand into the narrow opening left by the sword but that if he wanted to, he could thrust his whole arm through Jesus's body until his hand came out the other side.

15. The biblical accounts of Jesus's life are subject to every kind of error, as they were not written until many years after Jesus's death. Yet if we read between the lines of those accounts, it is clear that something happened shortly after the Crucifixion that changed the lives of Jesus's followers and of their followers after that. We will never know for sure exactly what it was, but something happened, and it changed the world forever.

The great chain of being assumes degrees of perfection. Every lower link in the chain brings one to greater imperfection until at last, at the atomic level, particles cannot even be depended upon to remain matter or energy. Yet Jesus, by all scriptural accounts the most perfect man who ever lived, is shown in those same Scriptures to be as unstable as a quark at the end of his earthly incarnation. How shall we account for this? Perhaps the great chain of being is not linear but circular, its lowest link connected to its highest, Ouroboros with its tail in its mouth, so that one can find no distinction between the properties at one end of the chain and those at the other. Or perhaps the chain sinks through ever-diminishing and unstable particles until it dissolves into the void out of which God's thoughts arise, the whole chain itself one thought that arises and subsides in the void.

According to Scripture, Jesus did not end his earthly existence in death. At the end, he was as insubstantial as a thought, as powerful as an idea, both matter and energy in the minds of his disciples whom he charged to continue his ministry. Something happened shortly after the Crucifixion. We will never fully understand what it was, but it changed the world forever.

One afternoon when a bunch of kids were playing in our yard, my father came out of the house and announced that he was walking up to the mansion. The Pied Piper's song could not have sounded sweeter to the children of Hamelin. For ten years the children of Hillhurst had lived in view of that house, never daring to trespass for fear of ghosts and vampires. No grown-up had ever expressed interest in the place. Now half a dozen kids danced in excitement as we followed my father up the side street that led to the mansion. At the end of that street was a little paddock with a small sagging stable at one end. The paddock was now nothing but a bramble. There were gaps in the fence; nothing lived there that wanted out, and no one outside had ever wanted in until that day. We waded through the bramble of the paddock and then pushed our way through the weeds to the top of the hill and over to the foot of the stone tower. It was empty, a vertical shaft of nothing, dimly lit by a small window at the top. What it ever could have been used for was a mystery. We quickly lost interest in the tower and walked over to the stone outbuildings. One was locked. Looking through the window, we saw what might have been a coffin among the other things stored inside. I made a mental note never to return after dark. The other buildings were empty and unlocked—two cottages of two rooms each, each room about four yards across. Nothing too remarkable there, so we turned back to the house. My father led us across the tall grass of the lawn and around the corner of the house where we gazed up, for the first time, at the white-columned facade of Hillhurst.

It was the most beautiful house I had ever seen. Better than Cheekwood, the stone house built in the 1930s where every year schoolchildren went on field trips to see the Christmas Trees of Many Lands. Better than the Hermitage, Andrew Jackson's mansion, and better than Belle Meade, both large and impressive tourist destinations that were marred by wide second-story verandas that cut off light and air to the porches below and spoiled the full Greek temple effect that I expected of a Southern plantation house. The facade of Hillhurst was perfectly proportioned. There was no second-story veranda. Instead, an elegant Juliet balcony was inset just above the wide front door, leaving the newly arrived visitor free to gawk at the full height of the thick white columns that towered from the bird shit on the floor to the peeling paint under the eaves.

Each of us tried the door; it was locked. We each tried again, jiggling the knob this way and that in the vain hope that the mechanism was just jammed. Then my father, who lifted weights and was greatly admired by the boys of my scout troop for the size of his arms, heaved his shoulder against the door. It flew open, not locked at all but just stuck from years of neglect. We were in.

Entering Hillhurst for the first time brought a feeling of déjà vu. We have all done this before. In our dreams, we have opened a door we never noticed and entered a room we never knew was there. Here, there was a whole house full of rooms: a mahogany-paneled library; a double-parlor with two marble columns and two marble fireplaces; a sun parlor with high, arched windows all around; a wide, carved staircase leading to a wide hall above, flanked by four corner bedrooms; a narrower staircase leading farther up to a nursery with sloped ceilings. Robinson or some previous owner had tucked a bathroom into the end of an enclosed back porch on the second floor, and there were electrical outlets throughout, but otherwise, the house was unimproved from its Civil War days. There were no coffins or any other furniture of any kind. The house was empty.

On the way home, my friends and I hung back from my father and the girls and made plans to visit the mansion again the next day. By the time I got home, I was already making plans to move in.

My friends were the boys who lived on my block, like Dennis, Robert and Keith, who lived in a row of houses across the street, and other boys, like Toby, who lived on our side of a hill that split our side of the neighborhood from the rest. I had known Dennis since I was three years old. We were not allowed to cross the street to play with each other at that age so we stood at the curb instead and threw rocks at each other, backed up by our little sisters, Kim on my side and Cathy on his. Dennis and I befriended Robert, Toby, and Keith, in turn, when they each moved into the neighborhood. We played as well on weekends with Larry, who stayed most weekends with his little sister, Tammy, at their grandparents' house two doors down from ours.

It was tacitly understood that whatever those boys might think of my increasingly evident gayness, they would never pick on me. "Evident gayness" means effeminate mannerisms. Kids never called me gay, a word they had never heard, or queer, a word they had. Queers were men who had sex with other men. The kids knew I wasn't having sex with anybody because they weren't having sex with anybody either. I was too young to be a queer. The word kids had for boys like me were "sissy" and "sweet," and when I prayed to Jesus to be cured of my homosexual feelings, implicit in those prayers was a desire never to hear those words again. There were other words I heard occasionally as well. "Momma's boys" was how our preacher's wife referred to her sons one morning at breakfast around a picnic table that my father, my brother, and I were sharing with the preacher's family on a church retreat. I had never seen a preacher angry before, but there was no denying that our pastor was very angry indeed when he said, "Grace, be quiet!" I don't think she knew what he was angry about. As far as she knew, she was only speaking the truth.

I discovered that the code of honor that protected me from being picked on in my own neighborhood existed in other neighborhoods as well. After joining Hillhurst, I became friends with David, the preacher's son who was closest to me in age. David lived in the parsonage behind the church, which was four blocks away, so we grew up playing with entirely different sets of kids. David would have been the poster boy of geek—tall and pale, with his black-rimmed glasses and flat-top haircut—were it not for the fact that he was as evidently gay as I was. We never talked about that. Our subject was science fiction. We sat together every morning on the school bus where, one day, he turned to me and asked if I had ever read *Lord of the Rings.* I replied that I had never heard of it. "Oh, it's great!" he said, "What happens is …" And for the next three months, I listened in a stupor as David described, in mind-numbing detail, every character and plot twist of that three-volume epic. Nonetheless, I liked David enough that I was willing to spend a week at a time in summer at his dining room table, which he and his older brother, Tom, had entirely covered with an enormous map of the world that they needed as a playing board for a highly advanced version of the board game Risk. Advanced Risk had taken them months to develop. They had gone far beyond conquering the world with little painted cubes of wood to represent troops. David and Tom had amassed nuclear arsenals that they unleashed with relish on each other and with undisguised glee on me. One day I was sitting there in a radioactive funk when in walked the boy whom I regarded as the most dangerous bully in Nashville.

His name was Kerry. Instead of pummeling us to death, Kerry took a seat and engaged David in conversation about some topic that they had clearly been discussing for years. My terror gradually subsided as I came to understand that Kerry, who lived nearby, and David had grown up together and therefore had the same improbable kind of friendship that I had with my sports-obsessed neighbors four blocks away. What was more, it appeared that because David was my friend, Kerry was extending immunity from his reign of terror to me as well.

The situation at school was far more perilous. It was one thing to have a girlfriend; everyone expected me to sit with her at lunch. It was another thing to risk all the respect I had stitched together with straight-As, two forensics trophies, and a Cougar Patrol sash by sitting at lunch with her—*and* with all her friends. Janet and her circle of childhood friends from Bellshire Elementary had all joined the forensics club, which was where I met them. I had attended a different grade school and had no childhood history with any of my lunchtime pals, except on days when we were joined by my lifelong best enemy, Barnetta Carter.

I had taken an instant liking to Barnetta when she transferred into Gra-Mar Elementary School. Our teacher that year helped our class make Christmas presents for our parents by shining the beam of a slide projector onto each of her pupils while she sketched the shadow of our profiles onto a sheet of paper taped to the blackboard behind us. We used the drawings to cut silhouettes of ourselves out of black construction paper that we then glued onto a white background, ready for framing.

I remember Barnetta's silhouette better than I remember my own—the impudent tip of her nose and the heartbreaking way her hair curled under just at her shoulders. I expressed my admiration for Barnetta by teasing and insulting her whenever I could, and Barnetta was always happy to return the favor. Part way through the school year, Barnetta was absent for over two weeks, something that had never happened to any other child that I could remember. I was worried. Her younger brother, Clayton, had been diagnosed with juvenile diabetes the year before. When Barnetta's diagnosis was confirmed, our teacher explained the disease and its treatment to us as best she could. Barnetta would have to give herself insulin shots for the rest of her life. I could not imagine injecting myself even once and worried even more until the morning Barnetta returned to school. She looked fine. I did not know what to say to her, so I told her that I was glad to see her. She reminded me what an idiot I was. I had never been so glad to hear it. Barnetta was fine. We settled back into our familiar routine of genial warfare.

The Bellshire girls did not insult me, but they also made it clear that I did not measure up to their ideal of manhood, which was okay with me since they were unable to articulate precisely what that ideal was. The difficulty lay in their inability to decide whether Rhett Butler or Ashley Wilkes was the dreamiest man ever. They all agreed, however, that Scarlett O'Hara represented the pinnacle of Southern womanhood, and they were each trying their best to emulate her, with varying degrees of success. The attempts that Janet, Karen and

Candy made at sharp-tongued sassiness were tart enough but were undermined by their readiness to dissolve into giggles at the least witticism from anybody. Beth Brown much more perfectly embodied the cool and enigmatic qualities in Scarlett that men found so fascinating, but I was not in a position to know that until I finally, after much nagging, agreed to read the book and see the movie. What a world opened up for me then! I suddenly had so much to talk about at lunch. I did not give a hoot about Rhett or Ashley, but I was mad for the furniture and the drapes. In my head, I began to decorate Hillhurst mansion just like the interiors of Tara and Twelve Oaks plantations. I also began to practice arching one eyebrow when I wanted to make a point, just like Scarlett. None of that was enough to upset the precarious balance I maintained between flamboyance and studious respectability, a balance that, along with the watchful eyes of the faculty, kept me safe from bullies. Then I made two disastrous social mistakes in rapid succession that put my life into a jeopardy from which even my elevated status on the Cougar Patrol might not save me.

Try to be more like Jesus. A tall order, indeed. How could those possibly be words to live by, given what the church tells us of the risen Lord, most perfect of men? I knew exactly what my mother meant when she told me to be more like Jesus because she spelled it out: hold your head up straight, don't fidget, say please and thank you. The preacher spelled it out, too, but in more exalted terms that were difficult to understand and even more difficult to put into practice. Here, it might be worthwhile to ask what Jesus himself expected his followers to do after he left them. The Gospels of Matthew, Mark, Luke, and John, as well as the book of Acts, all have something to say on the subject. In each, Jesus charges his followers with a mission, a charge that Christians take upon themselves to this day. Let us see how my own deeds stack up next to Jesus's expectations, as spelled out in the Scriptures.

The Gospel of Mark is universally accepted by scholars to be the oldest of the Gospels, so let us start there. In it, just before Jesus is received up into heaven, he admonishes his disciples, "Go ye into all the world, and preach the gospel to every creature." I am proud of my record on that charge. I was never told to be more like Jesus without my crawling under the bed to deliver the same advice to my cat, Charcoal. I once even tried to preach the Gospel to my turtle, Blue Toes. Unfortunately, this was done on the first and only occasion when the turtle was taken out for a walk. I hope that Blue Toes listened to my sermon carefully and preached the Gospel to all manner of creatures in his long turtle life. I do not know whether he did or not because I never saw the turtle again. I turned my head for one second and the turtle was gone. Green grass, green turtle, gone forever. I went looking for the turtle every day and kept his plastic dish for weeks, hoping that Blue Toes would return, until at last the plastic palm tree in the dish broke, and my mother discarded the dish behind my back.

The list of instructions that Mark says Jesus gave to his disciples is so long and so specific that it is hard not to think that a later writer snuck in some additions. The next item on the list is standard issue Christianity—be saved and baptized. I proudly point out that Baptists are careful to follow Jesus's instructions in the order that he gave them. I already have recorded my successes regarding these. As to the rest, I candidly confess dismal failure. Just before flying off to heaven, Jesus tells his disciples that the following activities will proclaim a Christian's holiness to the world:

- Snake handling
- Casting out demons
- Speaking in tongues
- Drinking poison without dying

There are Christians to this day who take Mark's Gospel as ... well, gospel ... and regularly tempt fate by including these sacraments in their worship services. I have never attempted to worship God in this manner, nor has anyone I have ever known. Baptists go stone blind whenever they come upon this passage in the Bible. They would go stone deaf, too, if they ever heard it preached from the pulpit, but they never do. Baptist preachers have always preferred the softer, safer, and more poetic version of Jesus's charge given in the book of Matthew. Luke is similarly nonspecific in the accounts he gives, both in his eponymous Gospel and the book of Acts, which he wrote as well.

Jesus's charge to his disciples is known as the Great Commission. The most well-known version is Matthew's:

"Go ye therefore, and teach all nations, baptizing them in the name of the Father, and of the Son, and of the Holy Ghost: Teaching them to observe all things whatsoever I have commanded you: and, lo, I am with you always, even unto the end of the world." That Baptists take the baptism commission seriously can be surmised by any reader who has persisted this far into these pages. Less well known is the Baptist enthusiasm for teaching all nations. There is little that thrills a Baptist more than talk of missionaries. As a child, I used to imagine missionaries standing shoulder to shoulder in a pot of boiling water, praying and singing hosanna, while heathens danced around the cauldron and stoked the fire beneath it. Since the Baptist church does not follow a liturgical calendar, the only high points of the religious year are revival (which can occur any time in warm weather), Easter, Christmas, and the Lottie Moon Christmas Offering, which supports Baptist missions around the world. The last is noteworthy because if one attends a large church like Grace Baptist, there is a good chance that a real live missionary will come and speak to the congregation about missionary work. I was never quite sure who Lottie Moon was, but I knew she had something to do with China. I somehow got her image confused with a photograph I once saw of Marlene Dietrich dressed as Shanghai Lily in the movie *Shanghai Express*. How I loved the special blue-and-white offering envelopes of the Lottie Moon Christmas Offering! How I loved to ignore the missionary while I drew pictures on the envelopes of Marlene Dietrich and Anna Mae Wong, singing hosanna in a pot of boiling water!

Implicit in the Great Commission is the idea that the benefits of knowing Jesus are too good to keep to yourself. The whole point of evangelism is evangelizing, or preaching the good news of Jesus's death and life (in that order) to as many people as will listen. Of course, most evangelicals do not evangelize themselves but have volunteered instead to listen from the pews. This does not mean, however, that they are off the hook for spreading the Gospel. There is a seldom spoken but nonetheless real acknowledgment among Baptists that you owe something to the person who was thoughtful enough to lead you to Christ. You have an obligation to that person, an obligation that is only fulfilled when you lead another person to accept Jesus as his Lord and Savior. I had owed that debt to my father ever since, one summer evening before supper, he asked if I wanted to become a Christian and then knelt with me by my bed while I asked Jesus to forgive my sins. From the moment I accepted Jesus as my Lord and Savior, I was obliged to my father to someday lead another soul to Christ.

"Witnessing" is what Baptists call the specific act of reaching out to a sinner with the offer of salvation through Jesus. The Lord laid it on my heart to fulfill my obligation to my father by witnessing to my friend Robert. Robert was a pigeon-toed and barrel-chested devil whose forelock was perpetually spilled between his slanted black eyes despite his constant attempts to rake or swing It back. We played together every afternoon after school, and when we got too old to play, we hung out instead while Robert told dirty jokes. Robert's father was inducting his son into an ancient tradition of oral literature by passing on to Robert a vast collection of dirty jokes that he heard all day long at the clinic where he ran the X-ray machine. Robert knew more dirty jokes than anyone I have ever known before or since. I later had occasion to recite as many of Robert's jokes as I could remember. It took an hour and a half. I suspected that the reason Jesus laid Robert on my heart was that he wanted to recruit the boy before Robert could write a book.

Jesus put me on the spot when he laid Robert on my heart. On the one hand, other than the gay porn movie that was unspooling in my head, I was a model Christian boy. On the other hand, like other boys I wanted to be cool so that the bullies would never throw eggs at the house and toilet paper into the trees on Halloween. I knew that I had to do what Jesus wanted because I had given my life to him. I hoped that Jesus would remember that I was very shy and that he would let me wait at least for the perfect moment. I prayed that Robert wouldn't die in a car accident and go to hell before that perfect moment came, which it did one Saturday night following a Just Us concert.

The Lord had laid it on the heart of our church pianist, Judy, to start a teenage gospel singing group at Hillhurst. We were called Just Us. The first song we learned as we gathered around the piano on a Sunday afternoon was a theme song that Judy had written to kick off our future concert:

Just us, God only has just us,

To do His holy will,

If we don't do it, who will?

Just us …

There were a dozen of us, ranging in age from thirteen to sixteen. Judy herself was no more than twenty-five. She was pretty and had a blonde beehive hairdo, which was all you could see of her over the piano. We learned another song, bought matching outfits, and sang in public for the first time at our Sunday night church service. The song Judy chose was the most popular gospel song of the day, made popular by the most popular gospel singing group of the day, the Oak Ridge Boys. "Jesus Is Coming Soon" was the prototype of the songs that would eventually comprise Just Us's repertoire.

Most of Just Us's songs were about heaven, or how to get there, or how great it will be once we get there, or, most important of all if you want to impel sinners to give their lives to Jesus, what will happen immediately *before* we get there. So many of our songs were about heaven, in fact, that I began to wonder if Just Us's secret message was that Christians would be better off dead. Not that any of us expected to die. What we expected, what all evangelical Christians profess to believe, was that Jesus would return at any minute and that when he did, we would ascend into the sky to meet him as he floated down to earth in a cloud of glory. "Jesus Is Coming Soon" was the epitome of a Just Us song because it contained all the themes about heaven mentioned above. A line-by-line reading of the song tells us the following:

1. The end-times are upon us. You can tell because there are so many problems.
2. America's freedom is at risk. This point does not follow logically from the first, but since we only sang the song in America, our audiences intuitively connected the second point with the first.
3. Obedience to God is the only viable course of action at such a time.
4. Therefore, we should try to be like the pilgrims.
5. Jesus will return to earth at any minute. Nobody knows exactly when.
6. This will be bad news for all the people who have not accepted Jesus Christ as their personal Lord and Savior. "Doomed" is how the song describes them.
7. The dead people will erupt from their graves, and the righteous ones will meet all the rest of us Christians in the sky.
8. From there, we will head on up to heaven.
9. Our troubles will all be over when we get there.
10. We will have no worries.
11. We will kiss this world good-bye, when …
12. We fly home to glory.

One of the original members of Just Us was Judy's little brother, Burt. Burt had received a set of drums the previous

Christmas. As drummer, he was not required to sing. Gospel music groups of the day were strictly divided into the trio (Singing Rambos), quartet (Blackwood Brothers), or quintet (Oak Ridge Boys)—or in the case of Just Us, the dodectet—who sang the songs, and the band who provided the accompaniment. There was, however, a drummer for one of the well-known groups who had been given a solo that he sang from his seat at the drums. Judy thought it would be great to have her brother do the same. Burt turned out to have a nice voice, and the song became a staple of our repertory. "I Wish We'd All Been Ready" describes the moment in the end-times when sinners realize that all the Christians have left the planet. I was particularly haunted by one image in the song: a woman hears a noise and looks over to her husband's side of the bed, only to find that she is alone. The song does not go on to say whether that woman was murdered or starved or simply trampled to death in the stampede of sinners trying to outrun the plague of locusts that precedes Armageddon. I would lie awake nights wondering what happened to that woman and thinking how she must have cursed herself for not accepting Jesus's offer of salvation, like her husband had done.

Judy's taste in music ran to the apocalyptic. You would think that someone would have noticed the disconnect between the grim portent of the songs and the sunny smiles of the teenagers who sang them, but if they did they were too kind to mention it. And the truth is, no one would have noticed. The Apocalypse, in which every sinner who has not already been starved or murdered will drown in a river of blood, can be conveniently overlooked by born-again Christians because we won't be there to see it. Not for us, the Apocalypse. What we get is the Rapture, that moment foretold in the book of Revelation when the last trumpet will announce the Second Coming of Christ, and born-again Christians will levitate through the air to meet Jesus as he descends in glory from heaven. Born-again Christians long to be living in the end-time in order to make that flight, oblivious to the horrific fact that we will share the skies with the corpses of every Christian who ever lived, whose graves will open up and release their contents into the heavens when the last trumpet sounds. Another of Just Us's favorite songs glossed over that gruesome fact when it proposed an interval between the sounding of the last trumpet and the moment of Jesus's arrival on earth, when happy Christians everywhere will quit their jobs, in a sort of "take-this-job-and-shove-it" moment, so they can line the streets and crane their necks for a first glimpse of Jesus. "The King Is Coming" was a specialty number since Judy inserted a key change toward the end and drafted my friend David, the preacher's son, to shout the song's title over and over while our best singer, Betty Jean, lobbed her high note over the final inspirational chorus.

Outwardly, I smiled just like all the other kids in Just Us while we sang "Jesus is Coming Soon," "I Wish We'd All Been Ready," and "The King Is Coming." Inwardly, I hoped that the predictions of Jesus's imminent return were off by at least a decade. I did not pray for Jesus to postpone his Second Coming—that would have been presumptuous—but I did pray harder than ever for him to cure me of homosexuality whenever our pastor preached a sermon on the book of Revelation. A church pew is uncomfortable at the best of times, but I never squirmed on one so much as I did when the end-times were preached. I was almost as scared of the Rapture as sinners were supposed to be of the Apocalypse. The Rapture marks the time when all prayer ceases because it will no longer serve any purpose. Once the Christian meets his risen Lord in the skies and is whisked off to heaven, what further need will there be for prayer? Once he has moved into his heavenly mansion, picked out his celestial furniture, and hung his eternal drapes, once he embarks on an eternity in which he will never grow old or sick and never want for anything, what would he pray for? If Jesus did not answer my prayer to be changed into a heterosexual boy before his Second Coming, my shame on Judgment Day would be unbearable. A sermon on the Rapture filled me with a dread that no amount of doodling could dispel, because it meant that my prayers had a deadline, a deadline with no specific date attached but that could easily be tomorrow or even the next moment. Never mind that I could not enjoy being an adolescent boy because my religion forbade me to have a boyfriend; I could not even enjoy my religion for the constant fear that Jesus would return before I was ready.

Our Sunday night debut in the "special music" portion of the service was a success. Soon we were asked to provide the special music for the morning service. Another triumph. We learned new songs. We bought new outfits. Soon Just Us was carrying its special blend of youthful enthusiasm and apocalyptic warning into churches all over middle Tennessee. We sang the special music at worship services, church socials, and revival meetings. Within a year of its founding, Just Us was performing once or twice a week besides meeting for weekly rehearsals. Judy booked us into any church that asked—and had a stage large enough to accommodate our growing number.

There were just a few things I would have to take care of before I could move into Hillhurst mansion. I would have to grow up, get a job, strike it rich, and find a wife who looked like Cybill Shepherd. All that would take awhile, but there were a few things that a boy with a pitiful allowance and an over-fertilized imagination could do right away. I got right to work. As my friends and I wandered through the mansion every day after school, I began to visualize my future life there. First I picked out colors for the rooms and imagined drapes to match. I claimed the library as my personal domain and filled it with books and heavy furniture. I decorated the double-parlor, the dining room, and the sun parlor. The kitchen I outfitted with the avocado-green appliances that were in vogue at the time. I allowed Cybill to furnish a small lady's parlor for herself, as it was too narrow to accommodate the bulky Victorian furniture that I wanted for myself. Then I divided up the bedrooms among their future occupants.

When my parents remodeled our house, they built themselves a bedroom as far away from their children as possible and put in a private bathroom as well. I followed their example by commandeering the large nursery on the attic floor of the mansion for Cybill and me. I converted a small room across the hall into a bathroom. This left four large bedrooms and one bathroom on the second floor. Here I hesitated. I knew that I wanted to have at least four kids. If I had only four, that would mean a bedroom apiece. My parents had wisely separated their squabbling children into individual bedrooms to increase the odds that we would all survive into adulthood. I knew that the number of children sharing a bathroom was unimportant since Kim, Miles and I spent as little time as possible in ours. Four seemed like a sensible number of children and a good use of the space. Cybill could give birth to a set of quadruplets and each child would have its own room.

On the other hand, I had twin second cousins on my mother's side and knew that children born together share an eerie telepathic bond that would probably make it unbearable to sleep in separate rooms. The four corner bedrooms were just large enough for three single beds. I therefore assigned a set of triplets to each bedroom. Cybill beamed her delight. I decided to make her even happier by knocking out windows in the stone tower and dividing the vertical space into three floors. I converted a small structure on the back of the tower into a bathroom. Then I set to work deciding how many children I could stuff into that space. The bedrooms in the tower would be a bit larger than those in the house. I had seen a movie called *Cheaper by the Dozen* and reasoned that two dozen would be a bargain, so I wedged a set of quadruplets into each floor of the tower. I had also heard of a movie called *The Dirty Dozen* but figured that one bathroom for twelve kids in the house and another for twelve in the tower would take care of that problem.

With the stone outbuildings furnished as guest cottages and the dilapidated stable restored for my sister's horse in exchange for an agreement to stop pestering me, the renovation was complete. My plans for the future were ready. Life was looking good. All I needed now was one small miracle from Jesus that would turn me into a heterosexual father for all those kids.

That miracle could not come fast enough at school. My first disastrous social mistake involved a fund-raiser for the cheerleaders, who announced a school-wide contest to guess how many beans were in a jar. Pressed up against the glass of that jar by the weight of the beans inside was a five-dollar bill. Five dollars was a lot of money in those days, and most of the kids at school entered the contest. I wanted the money, too. I had never amassed anything close to five dollars all at once and saw, in this contest, a chance to prove to my parents not only that their bookworm of a son could learn the value of a dollar but that he might actually amount to something someday. But before I continue with this story, a word about my brother, Miles.

Miles Mason Fields was named for Miles Mason Fowler, also called Bud, my grandfather who died in a car accident when my mother was a year old. Miles is four years younger than my sister, Kim, and six years younger than me. The age difference meant that for much of my childhood, Miles was either an adorable little imp or an aggravating nuisance. I watched his exploits from a distance of six years rather than participating in them directly. Not that I would have participated anyway. From an early age, Miles's idea of play was much too industrious to suit me. He planted his first garden at the age of five. That same year, he asked my father if he could have some scrap lumber that had piled up in a corner of the garage. My father absentmindedly said yes. A week later, my brother's cats, Ya Chai and Snowball, had a split-level mobile home with hinged windows that Miles had built to fit into the bed of his little red wagon. Thereafter, he would arrange his cats on the roof deck of their house and take them for a ride up and down the driveway every afternoon. That was when he realized just what a world of possibilities was open for a clever boy with a little red wagon. My sister had a horse that was kept at a stable a short drive from our house. Miles asked my father if he could shovel some horse manure into garbage bags. My father agreed to let him but only if Miles paid for the garbage bags himself, figuring that would be the end of it. But Miles had plenty of money even then because he saved the dime he got every week for his allowance and all the money he got for his birthday. Miles went to the store with Mama Fields and bought a box of thirty garbage bags. A week later, he had thirty bags of manure that he hauled around the neighborhood and sold as fertilizer. Who wouldn't give a dollar to buy a sack of turds off the little red wagon of an enterprising five-year-old boy with big blue eyes and freckles on his nose? Soon Miles had thirty dollars stashed away someplace where Kim and I would never find it. It was not long before he was lending money to his big brother and sister. Miles never let us forget how much money we owed him and said that the only reason he was not charging interest was that he could find no one who would teach him how to compute it.

I was not about to hazard my chances of winning the bean-counting contest on a wild guess. I needed that money to get out of debt. When the cheerleaders brought the jar around to the table where Barnetta, Beth, and I were sitting with our friends, I took my time with it. I wrapped a napkin around it, marked the spot where the ends overlapped, and then divided that length into ten equal measures. I visually marked out a slice down the side of the jar equal to one of those measures and counted how many beans were visible next to the glass along that slice and how many beans were visible in the triangle below it on the bottom of the jar. The cheerleaders were amused by all this, and neither they nor anyone else would have ever suggested that what I was doing might be cheating since no one at the school seriously believed that anything we were learning had any application whatsoever in the real world. Once I had counted the beans in the side section and the triangle below it, I multiplied those two numbers together, multiplied the resulting number by ten, and then announced to the world that there were 5,842 beans in the jar. There were 5,856. People talk. By the time I won the contest, everyone knew that I had derived my guess by calculation. Kids were furious. How, they wondered, was it fair that an honor student could use mathematics to deprive some average student of the five dollars that he or she had no other way of getting than by making a wild guess at how many beans were in a jar? I ignored the critics and regretted the words "sore losers" that flickered across the movie screen in my mind where Jesus was sure to notice them. With those five dollars in my pocket, I once again enjoyed the antics of my little brother, unencumbered by envy or debt. I also attracted the unwanted attention of a would-be school bully named Buck.

My second disastrous mistake came shortly after my triumph with the bean jar, when my sister and I performed in the school talent contest. We played a two-piano mash-up of tunes like "Twinkle Twinkle Little Star" and "Old MacDonald Had a Farm" that our piano teacher had insisted we learn so that we could perform for an association of piano teachers to which she belonged. If I were not so competitive by nature, I would have never suggested that we enter that contest playing such piffle. Kim had just been elected to the cheerleading squad and could afford to look like an egg-headed jerk for one afternoon. I could not.

Kim and I performed first. The audience of students and teachers assembled on the bleachers in the gym applauded politely when we finished. For an hour, we looked like the act to beat. Then the last act took the stage—a rock band that not only had the requisite guitars and drums but amplifiers to boot. The band had been assembled hastily, just a month before, with the express purpose of winning this contest. They knew one song, Three Dog Night's "Joy to the World." I recognized the first chords and thanked God that at least if we had to compete against a rock band, that band would be singing about a bullfrog, a song choice that made "Old MacDonald Had a Farm" seem a little less corny. When the band finished, the audience went wild. It had never occurred to anyone that an actual rock band could be scraped together out of the student body of Ewing Park Junior High School. The faculty panel of judges was in a pickle. Everyone preferred the rock band, even the faculty. Ewing Park was a brand new school, which meant that its faculty had been drawn from the recent graduating classes of schools of education. The faculty judges were no more than thirty years old and much more likely to spend their leisure hours listening to Three Dog Night than to "Twinkle Twinkle Little Star." Even Kim and I preferred the rock band. But the faculty panel could not ignore the years of training it took to play a two-piano duet. In the end, the judges voted their consciences and not their hearts. Kim and I accepted our first-place ribbons to a loud chorus of boos. I was more visible, more famous than ever.

Buck began to heckle me in the cafeteria lunch line. I had learned long before that if you are afraid of a dog, you must pretend that you are not and then the dog will not attack you. I tried the same tactic with Buck and it worked. Of course, it might have worked because Buck was not as mean as he wanted people to think he was. He was no bigger than I was, either. But his heckling, on top of all my newfound notoriety, was starting to attract the attention of boys who *were* bigger and who *were* meaner and whose mercy I had good reason to doubt. I had never noticed those boys before and they had not noticed me. Now they were giving me menacing looks and mouthing the words "sweet boy" when they passed me in the halls. I had to repair my reputation—and fast—if I wanted to escape the ninth grade without injury.

The first new members of Just Us were four boys from Donelson Baptist who played guitar and sang together. They were cool. They wore their hair longer than the boys at Hillhurst. Two of them had mustaches. They not only played the songs of Crosby, Stills, Nash & Young but sang them in perfect harmony. They were handsome and funny and brought a jocular quality to the group that had been missing. They inspired the rest of us to abandon top-forty radio and buy albums instead by the acoustic earth-hippie bands they favored. We boys devised ways to trick our parents into postponing our haircuts. We got our sisters to sew patches onto the blue jeans we wore to practice. Judy swapped out her beehive for a shoulder-length flip. As the sixties gave way to the seventies, we bought more outfits, this time in the shades of brown and beige that were the hallmark of that decade. Just Us was now the coolest place a young Christian could be. We attracted a couple more kids from other churches. Then Judy found Tommy, Donna, and Mary Lou.

Nobody ever quite understood where they came from. They knew each other but were not exactly friends. They did not seem to belong to any particular church. They appeared to come from some demimonde of Christian evangelism that was hidden from ordinary churchgoing folk. Tommy, Donna, and Mary Lou were different from the other kids in Just Us. The original members of Just Us were enthusiastic. These new kids were fervent. They were not just Christians. They were evangelists. Tommy's Bible seemed to be grafted to his hand. Donna was ethereal, the kind of Christian who truly does appear to glow from the light of God's love within. Mary Lou's sunny personality was a thin veneer for a steely determination to serve Christ wherever He might lead, and the gorier the journey, the better. They quickly raised the bar for bearing witness to Christ's message. Judy was the first to leap over the bar. Here, at last, was the beginning of the full-blown evangelical mission she apparently had in mind when she started Just Us. She began organizing outings for the group. We had always gone to gospel music concerts, but now we went out together whenever a famous evangelist was in town. One night we all went to a dimly lit house across town filled with hippies who were praying together when we arrived and still praying two hours later when we left, with no sign of ceasing to pray anytime soon. I never knew which member of Just Us it was who found that prayer meeting, but I am certain it was not one of the original twelve.

Our rehearsals changed. We had always rehearsed for two hours and then socialized over soft drinks and snacks before going home. Shortly after Tommy, Donna, and Mary Lou joined the group, Judy instituted a prayer circle between the rehearsal and the snacks. We would dim the lights in the room, sit in a circle, and join hands. Whoever was moved by the Spirit would pray aloud. I was always content just to listen while the others prayed; I never got comfortable praying out loud. The next change was in the performances themselves. One night Tommy stepped to the microphone between songs and delivered an impromptu message on the subject of God's love. Mary Lou said amen at the end of it. Soon anybody in the group might preach or pray without warning, to the accompaniment of more and more amens and hallelujahs. That the people who did so were almost always Tommy, Donna, or Mary Lou was okay with Judy, whose eyes shone as she watched, and with the rest of us as well, who were having trouble keeping up with the newfound fervor of our leader and her new recruits.

The last change in Just Us was, for me, the most frightening of all. Before each performance, Judy would ask one or two of us to give our testimony. "Giving your testimony" is what Baptists call telling the story of your conversion to Christianity. Alcoholics Anonymous has a similar exercise that they call "qualifying." In testimony, you give a brief synopsis of your life story with an emphasis on sin, and then relate in detail the moment you were born again. You then follow that with a quick roundup of all the ways your life is better now that you are walking with the Lord. Obviously, the best testimonies were those given by people who held high rank in Satan's army before finding Jesus. My parents once worked on a movie—my father designing the sets, as usual, and my mother recruited as wardrobe mistress—called *From Crime to Christ* that followed that formula. The protagonist of the story was an out-and-out hooligan with real crimes to his credit and thus deserving of an hour and a half of screen time. A less flagrantly criminal background could still be spun into an evangelical career, as happened with one popular evangelist of the time who would start every sermon by asking his audience if they "smoke-drink-cuss-swear-chew and run around with other people who do," as he had once done before giving his life to Jesus.

The first time Judy asked me to testify, she spun around in the pew in front of me and whispered her request about five minutes before we were to take the stage. This did not leave me much time to prepare, but I did not panic. Not for nothing was I a mainstay of the school forensics and drama clubs.

I had given my share of extemporaneous speeches, and I was not about to flounder around on stage in some impromptu nightmare. While everyone else prayed silently to Jesus to bless our performance, I went to work cobbling together some sort of script in my head. I quickly rejected the idea of telling the congregation about the porn flick that played on a continuous loop in my head. I also realized that my actual sins were not going to make much of a story—who wanted to hear about the five-year-old who stole a rock from Danny Darby's rock collection? When the dreaded moment came, I first confessed that I did *not* smoke-drink-cuss-swear-chew or run around with other people who did. The congregation laughed at the reference. I was off to a good start. All my life I had listened to my family tell one tall tale after another and I put all that listening into the service of the Lord. I made a mountain out of a molehill of trivial sins. The congregation laughed. They chuckled. They chortled. Judy beamed. Right under her nose, all along, had been the clown act she needed to round out the evangelical circus that Just Us had become. From that night on, she asked me regularly to give my testimony. I never changed one word of it.

My attempts to be like Jesus were going beautifully in one respect: my relations with the opposite sex were chaste. I had not had a response from Jesus to my prayer for heterosexuality. This kept me out of trouble with the girls but was becoming awkward in my fantasy life. My two dozen children were growing up fast, yet I was not willing to think too carefully about just how they had been conceived. Ordinarily I prefer my fantasy life to be richly detailed. By now I had decorated the mansion down to the last curtain tie. I had provided a Japanese screen in the bedroom behind which Cybill could dress. Or undress. At which time the movie in my head would fade to black, adding no footage at all to the lurid documentary of my mental sins that I so dreaded seeing on Judgment Day. Cybill didn't seem to mind. I thought of Mary Magdalene, waiting patiently for Jesus to ask her out on a date. I thought of Jesus, irresistibly drawn to the woman with the shady past, wanting to be close to her but unable to find the words to explain to her just how complicated he was. Cybill could have been giving virgin birth for all she cared, just as long as she had a big, loving family around her.

I, however, was not willing to settle for a miraculous explanation for the presence of all these kids. If these kids were the result of virgin birth, then I had twenty-four Messiahs on my hands. That did not appeal to me. I was not interested in world domination. I just wanted to decorate the house and pick out groovy names for the kids. I started to cast about for other ways to explain the conception of my two dozen children. Science seemed promising, at first. Our set of *World Book Encyclopedia* offered little advice on the subject of miraculous reproduction, and I was too lazy to go to the library. Finding science no help, I turned to science fiction. If UFOs did exist, and I was pretty sure they did, the aliens inside would want to conduct experiments on Cybill and me after they abducted us. I picked out a field by the mansion that was large enough to land an alien spacecraft and imagined our terror as Cybill and I were forced on board at gunpoint (lasers!). I had gotten an A+ in science class and used all that knowledge to imagine a race of space aliens who needed desperately to find a way to create children out of thin air before their race died out. The aliens were careful to erase our memories when the experiments were over. The next morning Cybill and I wandered back up to the house, disoriented but somehow happier than we had ever been.

In late winter of the ninth grade, our glamorous speech-class teacher, Nancy Hamer, announced tryouts for a school play. We had performed plays around the desks in our speech and English classes, but this would be the first mounting of an actual school play at Ewing Park. My girlfriends and I were thrilled. Nancy Hamer was a real actress. She had lived and studied acting in New York City for several months before fleeing back to the South after getting mugged for the third time. Under the direction of a professional, the play was sure to be good.

I wanted the lead role of Jesse Stuart, the teacher in a one-room Kentucky schoolhouse who wrote the book upon which the play, *The Thread That Runs So True*, was based. I figured I had a good chance of getting it, having made a name for myself as an actor with my performance as the nervous suitor in Anton Chekov's one-act *The Marriage Proposal.* When I lost the role of Jesse Stuart, Ms. Hamer explained to me, as tactfully as she could, that the role required the actor to participate in a fistfight with my friend Tommy Sims, an extremely tall student who had been cast in the role of Jesse Stuart's rival for the affections of the only pretty girl in the one-room school. My heart sank. The only time I had ever been in a fight was with Tommy Sims, on the playground in second grade. Tommy had pushed me into a mud puddle and that was the end of the fight. The role of Jesse Stuart went to Eric Bischoff, the other male star of speech class. Being a drama star had done nothing to tarnish Eric's reputation for manliness since he was also a star athlete. He was very gener-ous as well. Just before the start of rehearsals, Eric stopped me in the hall and told me that he had withdrawn from the play. The role of Jesse Stuart was mine. He cited some athletic competition or other as his reason for withdrawing. Whatever his reason was, he could not disguise how happy it made him to give me something he knew I really wanted.

The fight scene took several afternoons to block. Ms. Hamer made sure that I kept my wrists locked and that my movements did not look too graceful or balletic. Just before the play opened, I had the actor's nightmare of being onstage without a line. I need not have worried. The play was a suc-cess. The cast was enormous, requiring enough kids to fill a schoolroom, which meant that there were many parents, family members, and friends in attendance. We performed the show for three nights to sold-out audiences. At the climax of the play, I could hear the ooohs and aaahs of the audience as Tommy and I broke up the schoolroom in our carefully choreographed fight.

The next Monday, I braced myself in the cafeteria lunch line when I caught sight of Buck, who was making his way down the line behind me. "That fight looked real," he said when he drew up beside me. "Reckon you could do that in real life?" I was asked that question many times over the next couple of weeks. Nobody ever volunteered to find out if I could do that in real life. I escaped the ninth grade uninjured, thanks to the painstaking direction of an actress who would have been in New York City had she not been mugged so many times.

Just Us's first and only concert took place at Hillhurst. After two years of rehearsal, performance, and prayer, Judy decided that we were polished enough to provide a Saturday evening's entertainment. For the first time, Just Us would perform as a solo act unattached to any regularly scheduled event like a church service or a revival meeting. Judy reckoned that Just Us might reach some sinners on a Saturday night that we might never reach on a Sunday morning. It was a gamble, since we were asking our families and friends to come out and support us on the one night of the week when they felt entitled to be anywhere other than church. The gamble paid off. My friend Robert would never have come to church on a Sunday, but like any fourteen-year-old boy, he was looking for something to do on a Saturday night. I invited him to come hear us sing. When Just Us filed out onto the stage, I scanned the audience and saw Robert's face in the pews for the first time, way in the back where the bad kids sat.

Just Us had a large repertory by then. All we had to do to please the crowd was stay on key and show off our new outfits. But by that time, Just Us was much more than just a singing group, and that night we pulled out all the stops. Tommy brandished his Bible and preached. Donna prayed for the world. Mary Lou stepped up to the mike with no idea what she would say once she got there and ended up describing the Crucifixion. The fact that she had not seen it herself did not stop her from describing it in grisly detail ("His back looked like hamburger!"). Judy cut the Crucifixion short with a loud chord, and we cheered everybody up with a bouncy rendition of "Jesus Is Coming Soon." I assured the crowd that I still did not smoke-drink-cuss-swear-chew or run around with anybody else who did, despite the fact that Robert was sitting in the back row. We sang more songs. David shouted, "The King is coming!" Burt wished we'd all been ready. Betty Jean deafened the crowd with her high note. We all stayed on key. There were two encores, both carefully planned. Southern Baptists do not applaud in church, but they applauded that Saturday night. "Amen," "Praise the Lord," and "Hallelujah" rang out across the sanctuary. Just Us was a hit.

After the concert, after our families and the other members of the audience were gone, Just Us had a prayer circle by the altar. Robert had stayed on since he planned to walk home with me, so he was included in the circle as well. It turned out that the concert had been only a warm-up act for the Holy Spirit, who moved mightily through that prayer circle. This was the moment that Jesus had led me to, I knew. I tapped Robert on the shoulder and asked him if he wanted to pray. He said yes. I got up and led him to an empty pew a ways off from the altar. There I guided Robert through the well-known steps to salvation that were outlined in the back of the pamphlets I so loved. Robert accepted Jesus into his heart. Afterward we rejoined the prayer circle and told them what had happened. Just Us rejoiced. Robert whooped. Judy beamed. Here was undeniable evidence that Just Us was indeed making a difference in the world, one soul at a time.

That Saturday night concert was the pinnacle of Just Us's success, though we did not know that at the time. By then, the group had grown so large that it was bound to collapse of its own weight. Things began to go sour. The Donelson boys started skipping the prayer circles after rehearsal, going straight to the snacks table after the singing stopped. I heard one of them mutter the words "rain dance" as he left the room. Tommy, Donna, and Mary Lou began missing rehearsals and performances as they walked farther along the winding paths to Jesus that had brought them to us in the first place. Judy left Hillhurst and joined another church. After rehearsal one night, Judy told us to pray for each other one last time, as God had laid it on her heart to disband the group. The members who were left were heartbroken. We were not only without a mission but without a social life as well. For two years, when we weren't rehearsing or performing, we socialized together. We dated each other. Our lives had revolved around Just Us.

Other changes followed hard on the breakup of Just Us. I transferred to another school, leaving behind the kids I had gone to school with since the age of six. I didn't see Robert so much anymore either, even though he lived just down the street. I do not know whether he ever published a compendium of dirty jokes, but it doesn't matter. He was baptized in a Baptist church. I can ask him about it in heaven.

There is no Great Commission at the conclusion of the Gospel according to John. Instead, there is a rather frosty dialogue between Jesus and Peter concerning John, "the disciple whom Jesus loved." Peter asks Jesus something to the effect of "What's to become of him?" Jesus's reply is something on the order of "If I want him to stick around until the Second Coming, what's that to you?" This is not the first reference in the Gospels to the disciple whom Jesus loved. The references are puzzling. The implication is that Jesus was capable of loving some people more than others. A Jesus who could love some people more than others is hard to reconcile with a Jesus who is reported to have said, "Love thy neighbor as thyself." If we are to love our neighbors as ourselves, is it a stretch to believe that Jesus was also asking us to love all men equally? If Jesus was God, and "God is love," surely Jesus loved everyone as mightily as possible. If that is the case, why single out one particular disciple as the beloved of Jesus? Is it possible that there truly was a special relationship between Jesus and that disciple?

Did Jesus have a boyfriend? Much has been made in recent years over the speculation that Jesus may have been the lover of Mary Magdalene and that she may indeed have been his wife and even the mother of his child. Certainly the Bible places her prominently on the scene at Jesus's Resurrection. As homosexuality has only recently become a love that dare speak its name, it is little wonder that less ink has been spilled over the speculation that Jesus may have been dating one of his disciples. Was John, the beloved disciple, actually Jesus's boyfriend? It is unlikely that the fragmentary Gospels still hidden in the crockery of the Roman Empire will ever supply us with an answer to this question. But no matter. For now, we can be grateful at least that the Gospels of the New Testament have supplied us with the question.

I did not have a boyfriend. What I had was Larry. Larry was a cinnamon-haired boy with a wicked grin and a fondness for blackmail. His grandparents lived two doors down the street from us. Larry stayed with them every weekend and most of the summer. He went to a different school from the other kids in the neighborhood but went to church with me on Sundays. I seldom saw Larry during the school week but would speak to him on the phone when he would call to talk about his muscles. I never tired of hearing about his workout routines and rejoiced with him when he called one night to say that he had just been elected Most Muscular Boy in the School.

Larry and I often arranged sleepovers at his grandparents' house or ours. We had a favorite game that we would play after everyone else had gone to sleep, which could only be played in our underwear. We would each pick a part of the other's body and take turns brushing our fingertips over it. The goal of the game was to be rubbed as lightly as possible without getting tickled or laughing. One night, Larry observed that we had rubbed everything there was to rub except the bottom of each other's balls. Upon hearing that, Pinocchio rolled over and pretended to fall asleep, knowing perfectly well that if he tried to pass himself off as a real boy while having the bottom of his balls rubbed by the Most Muscular Boy in the School, it would not be his nose that would grow until his lie was exposed. The problem here was not that I was uninterested in exploring Larry's genitals or in having him explore mine. In fact, few regions on earth were more interesting to me than Larry's nether parts. The problem, as I saw it, was that I could not afford to add any more footage to that great celestial movie of my life that would have its premiere on Judgment Day. The next time we had a sleepover, I told Larry that I was tired of midnight tickle rubs. From then on, we contented ourselves with pillow talk.

On the surface, things were going well for Cybill and me. Our oldest quads were graduating from Harvard. The next set were poised to release their first rock 'n' roll album, while the third had just qualified for the Olympics. Life was sweet. The only fly in the ointment was that I had not yet told my wife about my special relationship with the boy in math class.

His name was Paul. This boy was entirely one color, that color being the nutshell brown of his smooth skin, his steady eyes, and the bangs cut straight across his forehead. I had never met him. I never would meet him if I could help it. God only knew what shade of vermillion would blaze up my face if he ever shook my hand. The relationship existed only in my head, like just about everything else in my life. It was real nonetheless, in the sense that I thought of little else. My attention was riveted upon that boy every day from ten to eleven o'clock, so much so that I made a C+ in math for the first time in my life. It was not that I wanted to be his boyfriend; I certainly did not want to have sex with him. I just wanted to spend every waking minute with him. I wanted a telepathic bond with him that made talking unnecessary. I wanted to merge my life completely with his. In short, I wanted to *be* him … almost. Almost but not quite. I wanted to be just separate enough from him that there would be two of us instead of one, so that we could spend our whole lives together in telepathic union instead of just being one person.

Also, my grades were higher than his, so financially I really could not afford to be Paul. If I wanted to go to college, which I did, I needed to regain my position as champion of the honor roll or there would be no scholarships. I tried to put Paul out of my mind. That was impossible. Even Jesus was no help. I couldn't study harder, so I just studied longer. Spring came, sweaters were swapped for short-sleeve shirts, and I discovered that Paul was not the only fish in the sea. I got an A in math. Summer came and with it, the end of my special relationship with the boy in math class. I never met him. The next fall I enrolled at another school. A bigger sea, with many more fish in it.

My prayer campaign to Jesus wasn't going so well. In fact, it wasn't going anywhere at all. This did not seem fair. After all, it was Jesus himself who said, "Ask, and it shall be given you." I had fulfilled my side of that bargain but had not received even a moment's respite from homosexuality. Again, this did not seem fair. Measured against the Great Commission, I had not done too badly. Teaching all nations was a stretch for a kid who did not even have a driver's license, but I had given my testimony all over middle Tennessee while performing with Just Us. I had led my best friend to Christ. Yet I was still beset with sexual desires that would one day wreck my plans to get married and have quadruplets. All I could think was that I wasn't trying hard enough. That's about all any Christian can think when his prayers go unanswered. Since all things are possible with God, any fault for unanswered prayers must lie with us. And according to our preachers, if there is a fault, it is always this: lack of faith. If we only have faith, we are taught, God will work miracles in our lives.

This left me in a quandary. How was I to have more faith? I was already sure of God's existence and of his power to remake me in his heterosexual image. What additional faith was possible, then? Having more faith is easy to say in the pulpit but difficult to do in the pew. If you've spent your whole life praying and reading Sunday school lessons and singing hymns and listening to Bible stories and doodling through sermons, there isn't much more Jesus to be had. The stalwart Christian is thus left with little means of increasing his faith beyond praying over and over while repeating to himself, "I believe, I believe, I believe." That was pretty much what Dorothy did to get back to Kansas. But as *The Wizard of Oz* teaches, repeating your prayer while focusing intently on your belief is not enough to guarantee success. You must wear red shoes. The Good Witch must wave her wand. Some magic, some divine intervention, is required.

The only prayer that is always answered is the prayer for forgiveness of sins and salvation through the blood of Jesus Christ. After that, the man of faith will spend the rest of his life wondering why his neighbor's prayer was answered while his own was ignored. I had done my share of praying and had noticed that a prayer sent to heaven had about the same effect on the course of my life as a stone thrown into the water has on the course of a river. Prayers for all kinds of improvements were sent up to heaven all around me every day and yet the world went on pretty much as it had always done. I could not help but notice that God seemed to be very picky about which prayers he answered.

Santa Claus was more reliable. Santa could be counted on to bring me most, if not all, of the things I wanted for Christmas, and that seemed to be true for other kids whose fathers were employed. Each year, my parents very thoughtfully helped me to edit my Christmas list so that by December 24, the items on the list were a close match to those piled under the tree the next morning. Disappointments were few. I once asked for a rifle just like the Rifleman's and received a plastic facsimile that could be cocked and fired with one smooth motion of the hand; it was just like Lucas McCain's except that Santa had refrained from loading mine with bullets. Santa's policy seemed to be that any request would be granted, as long as it was not too expensive, would fit under the tree, and would not place my siblings in danger.

God, however, seemed to be running a very different kind of operation that most closely resembled a movie studio. Those studios maintain "slush piles" where unsolicited manuscripts molder until they are eventually read. The odds that an unsolicited manuscript plucked out of the slush pile will be made into a motion picture are slim but are probably better than the odds that God will pluck and answer your prayer out of the millions that are floated up to heaven every minute from every corner of the globe. Given the apparent odds of receiving an affirmative answer to a prayer, I began to think that, in the absence of ruby slippers or a magic wand, luck might be more important than faith. I had little faith in luck. My hope was fading fast.

Satan was everywhere. Larry bought himself a T-shirt made of a loose-weave netting that reminded me of the nets the gladiators used in the movie *Spartacus*. I knew that a well-raised young man from the artisan class of Christianity such as myself must never wear such a concoction. I had to admit, though, that the shirt showed Larry's physique to great advantage. Once he acquired it, I began to look forward to our motorcycle rides together.

Larry was only fourteen years old when Santa heaved a motorcycle down his chimney. Larry's parents had more sense than Santa and quickly limited the amount of fun Larry could have on the behemoth. The rules for riding were (1) only on weekends, which meant that the motorcycle stayed in his grandparents' garage, just two doors down from our own; (2) only in Hillhurst subdivision and even then, only on the five streets closest to our own; and (3) only up to a certain speed, which was twenty-five miles an hour in front of his grandparents' house and fifty miles an hour as soon as he was out of earshot. None of the other boys in the neighborhood had a motorcycle or particularly wanted one, which meant that if Larry was to have anyone with whom to share his joy, someone must ride with him on the back of his. As far as I know, he never asked anybody but me.

As you might imagine, even at that reckless age, I had little use for speed and no use at all for noise and fumes. I politely declined Larry's first invitation to be squired around the subdivision on his screaming hog, but he would not take no for an answer. I wondered, as I reluctantly climbed aboard, whether I would have an open- or closed-casket funeral, and I praised God's everlasting mercy when an hour later, Larry dropped me off at the top of the driveway, dazed but unharmed. I swore to myself that I would never ride that motorcycle again, but when Larry showed up again the next weekend in his Spartacus shirt, the protests I had rehearsed all week suddenly seemed unsportsmanlike. I did ask if he would be warm enough in that shirt and he said yes. Well, why wouldn't he? He knew perfectly well that I would be clinging to him for dear life. With my arms wrapped tightly around him, the Most Muscular Boy in the School could have ridden naked through Hillhurst subdivision in perfect comfort. That thought did cross my mind, where it was instantly added to the feature-length documentary film of my sins. You will see it with the rest of mankind on Judgment Day.

Satan was everywhere. The documentary film of my mental sins was now so long that it could not be shown without an intermission. My prayer campaign to Jesus was not going well at all.

What are homosexuals made of, that we should be impervious to the power of prayer? Stern stuff, it seems. Are homosexuals men of steel? Or something so wispy it cannot be grasped long enough to be changed, like smoke? What did Jesus see when he looked down from heaven at the freckled kid with the unruly hair who begged him for a miracle? Something that he was powerless to change? Or something that he would never want to change, like a sunbeam, like laughter, like clear water?

Santa, Gepetto, and God go into their workshops. Santa takes a hunk of plastic and fashions it into this year's must-have toy. Gepetto takes a block of wood and a ball of twine and makes Pinocchio, not a real boy but real enough to wish that he were. What material does God take in hand when he wants to make a homosexual, who once made will remain as God has fashioned him?

The homosexual knows that he never became a homosexual, that homosexuality is not something that is acquired, like a taste for scotch. The homosexual knows that he was always homosexual. It was not *Wonder Woman* comics that I subscribed to with my small savings before I could even read; it was the Martian Manhunter. The homosexual, looking back, knows that he was always homosexual, that no flaw was ever introduced into the design. Was he then flawed from the start? Born less perfect than his heterosexual friend? At what time could the homosexual be said to have become imperfect?

If the universe is created out of the perfect material, and if it was created by the perfect being beside whom no other existed, when did that perfect material become imperfect enough to make a homosexual? Or a Hitler, or an avalanche, or a flaw in a diamond? How does something that is perfect acquire its first imperfection? Two possibilities present themselves. The first is that God himself desired the first mistake and therefore created it. One could make the argument that the world was perfect until the first homosexual appeared in it. Let us say then, just for the sake of argument, that God, the perfect being, evinces a perfect desire to introduce the perfect mistake into the perfect substance by sending a homosexual down to the army recruiting center. Since the mistake originated in perfection and is therefore itself a perfect mistake, is it fair to regard it as a mistake at all? Or if one grants that this perfect mistake is in fact a mistake, does it not simply take its place alongside all the other manifestations of God's will in the ranks of perfect mistakes? Call the homosexual a mistake then, if you will, but do not call him imperfect. Just teach him to fire a rifle and polish his boots, and he will take his place in the ranks of perfect things.

The second possibility is that God, the perfect being, evinced a perfect desire to introduce a perfect and unending kaleidoscope of changes into the perfect substance. Call those changes mistakes, decay, or suburban sprawl; call them progress, improvements, or real estate development; call them what you will, but consider the possibility that God never regarded anything created out of perfection as anything other than perfect. What changes is still perfect. What is different from other things is just another perfect manifestation of God himself. And what does not change remains perfect just as it is, just as God made it.

What did Jesus see when he looked down from heaven at the freckled kid with the unruly hair who begged him for a miracle? Something that could not be changed? Or something that he preferred just the way it was? My prayers to be changed into a real boy went unanswered. Or perhaps it would be more accurate to say that they were answered, and the answer was that God had no wish to change a boy in whom he was well pleased.

One bright Sunday morning when Larry and I were walking back home from church, his little sister, Tammy, came running toward us down the street. Her pale blonde hair flapped in her wake, and her face was stricken. The news she carried broke our hearts, broke the heart of every child in Hillhurst subdivision. The mansion was gone. It had burned to the ground in the middle of the night. Had any of us been awake in the wee hours, we would have seen the flames. No one knew what caused the fire, whether it had been accidental or intended, and if intended, what motive there might have been for setting it. After lunch, my father walked with us and the other kids in the neighborhood up the hill to the spot where the mansion had been. A couple of the walls were still standing, too thick to fall, white no longer, just rough red brick. Everything else was gone.

A collective depression settled over the children of Hillhurst subdivision. I did not know how the other kids had populated that house in their own imaginations, but evidently they had. I did not move my own imaginary family into another house. Instead, I grieved for the loss of the whole built-up fantasy. The house, the decorations, the wife, the children, the whole sweet imaginary life I had lived in that place dissipated like so much smoke.

My friends and I no longer had the heart to visit the site where the mansion had been. We did not go up to play in the outbuildings that remained. No one ever found out how the fire started. Eventually the stone cottages were knocked down. Today an apartment complex stands on the site. It is called Hillhurst.

I turned sixteen a year ahead of Larry and got a driver's license; that brought an end to motorcycle riding. My parents bought another car so that I could drive out of our district each morning to the magnet school where I could take drama classes in a theater lab and astronomy classes in a planetarium. I made new friends. Rich Acres Drive, with our house at one end and our church at the other, was no longer the axis of my world. The other kids from Just Us joined the church choir. I had a choice to make. Choir rehearsals were on Wednesday nights, and so were rehearsals for the plays I wanted to act in at school. I won a small role in *Our Town*. The next Sunday, from the back pew, I watched my Just Us friends take their seats in the choir, while I sat in back with the rowdy kids, who dropped pictures of naked ladies into the offering plate and gave no thought at all to what people would say about them on Judgment Day.

On a Sunday night in summer, I sent up to Jesus my last, final, ultimate prayer that I might be as other boys were. By this time I had no reason to believe that my request would be granted, so I phrased my prayer in the form of a bargain: if I woke up gay on Monday morning, I would assume that it was God's will, and I would put my faith in him to make things turn out well. The bargain stands to this day. I never asked to be heterosexual again.

THE CHURCH OF MAN

"Man's last and highest parting is when, for God's sake, he takes leave of God." —*Meister Eckhart, fourteenth-century German preacher and mystic*

This is a story about the kingdom of heaven and one gay man's search for it, starting in the Southern Baptist Church into which I was born. As you might suspect by now, I am no longer a member of that church. The steps I took away from it are the subject of Part Three.

Mark 1:9, 12:

And it came to pass in those days that Jesus came from Nazareth of Galilee and was baptized of John in Jordan.
And immediately the spirit drove him into the wilderness.

When I was eighteen years old, despite overwhelming sexual longings, I resolved that I would never, ever go to bed with a man. Unless he was David Bowie.

When I was seventeen years old, it occurred to me that the little Indian boy who got all those leftovers from my mother must now be about my size. It also occurred to me that maybe he wasn't going to hell after all.

When I was sixteen years old, my friends Barnetta Carter and Beth Brown and I took seats with two dozen strangers around the stage of a small laboratory theater at Belmont College. We were there for an experimental theater workshop called the Body Shop. It was to be co-led by the drama teacher at the new magnet school where my friends and I would begin classes in just a few weeks. The flyer announcing the Body Shop featured a reproduction of the Vitruvian Man, Leonardo da Vinci's famous drawing of a naked man whose four legs and four outstretched arms are inscribed within a circle and a square. The Vitruvian Man is Leonardo's attempt to describe the perfect proportions of the human body and, by extension, the perfect harmonies of all creation as well. Leonardo's drawing is a Renaissance illustration of the famous statement made by the Greek philosopher Protagoras: "Man is the measure of all things."

The seats of the theater were filled when a stocky man in his mid-thirties stepped onto the stage. He had the balding head, rounded belly and pleasant smile of a Buddha. Next to him was a lithe and exotic woman with olive skin and long dark hair, also in her thirties. The man smiled pleasantly and in a clear tenor voice said, "Welcome to the Body Shop. My name is Kent Cathcart." In a resonant bass, the woman next to him said, "And I am Ruth Sweet." That, for me, was the moment when school ceased to be a long slog through endless classes, exams and pep rallies. From that time on, high school would be a magic carpet ride through the artistic demimonde of Nashville, a ride launched each morning from a laboratory theater classroom at McGavock Comprehensive High School, called S-01.

Belmont College (Belmont University, now) is built around an antebellum mansion also called Belmont, a print of which hung in our living room, one of a limited edition made from a pen-and-ink drawing the college commissioned from my father. Belmont is a Christian university that until 2007 was supported—some might say controlled—by the Tennessee Baptist Convention. Clearly, the Baptist trustees of Belmont College were not aware of the freewheeling theatrical experiment going on in the little theater on campus that day in 1972.

Belmont is one of about twenty colleges and universities in and around Nashville. The number of institutions of higher learning in Nashville, as well as the prevalence of classical architecture to be found there, long ago earned Nashville the nickname "Athens of the South." Other nicknames are the

"Protestant Vatican" and "Buckle of the Bible Belt." In addition to over seven hundred churches, a visitor to Nashville will find several seminaries and religiously affiliated colleges and universities, as well as the publishing houses of the Southern Baptist Convention and the United Methodist Church. The city is home to the Southern Baptist Convention, the National Baptist Convention and the National Association of Free Will Baptists, and a good part of the administrative offices of the United Methodist Church are located there as well. Nashville's famous Music Row is the epicenter of the Christian pop and rock music industry, and the Gospel Music Association and the Gospel Music Hall of Fame are also located nearby. Nashville is home to Thomas Nelson, the world's largest Christian publisher and the world's largest producer of Bibles, as well as to Gideons International, the organization that places those Bibles on the nightstands of America's motels, hospitals, nursing homes and prisons.

Today, though, you are more likely to know Nashville by another nickname: "Music City USA." Nashville is famous the whole world over as the home of a weekly country music stage concert called the Grand Ole Opry. The Grand Ole Opry began in 1925. It is broadcast every week by WSM-AM and is the longest-running radio show in America. In the 1960s, when I was still a child, the popularity of country music made Nashville the second-largest producer of music in the country after New York City. In those days, Nashville had some of the feel of a company town. Country music was everywhere. No matter who you were, where you lived or what you did for a living, you had some connection, however tenuous, to the country music business.

My family didn't care for it. My father listened to opera. Annelle preferred orchestral music. We kids—me, my sister Kim, my brother Miles, and our cousin Rick otherwise known as "you kids" when our elders were about to issue a warning—listened to Top 40. But whatever your listening preferences, you could not tune out country music entirely. Every Saturday afternoon I would come into the house and turn on the television, hoping that this would be the week when the programmers decided to run cartoons all day long instead of stopping at noon. Every Saturday afternoon I was once again greeted by the grinning faces of Porter Wagoner and his costar, Dolly Parton. There was no use turning the channel since there was country music on every one, but I tried it every Saturday anyway. My grandmother Nanny would do the same thing with the radio dial in her red-and-white 1957 Chevrolet. We kids spent many of our childhood weekends in the backseat of that car while Nanny fidgeted with the radio, trying to find music that we wouldn't complain about. Most of those days we were out touring the lots where mobile homes were sold. Nanny had a perfectly comfortable 1920s bungalow four blocks from Grace Baptist Church, but her grandchildren had decided that she would be better off in a trailer. She wasn't about to trade her house for a trailer but she humored us, knowing she was better off letting us run wild through those trailers than keeping us at home where we could tear up her house.

When we weren't looking at trailers, we went to parks. Usually we went to Shelby Park, which was the closest park to Nanny's house and which had a merry-go-round whose axle was so greased that a group of kids could spin it fast enough to make ourselves nauseated. But sometimes when Nanny had had enough of trailers and merry-go-rounds, she would pile us into the back of the car and drive us through downtown to see the sights of Centennial Park. First she would take us to see the fighter jet mounted at one end of the park. Then she would watch, with her arms folded across her stomach, while we played pirates on a concrete replica of a ship's prow. Once we were exhausted enough to be trusted, she would take us to see the formal gardens and the magnolias. Then, last but best of all, we went to see the Parthenon.

Fans of the filmmaker Robert Altman will remember that in the last scene of his classic 1975 movie *Nashville*, Barbara Harris sings "It Don't Worry Me" under a giant American flag draped across a Greek temple, to a crowd of terror-stricken tourists running from a maniac who has just opened fire on country music's elite who are gathered there in celebration of some boondoggle or other. If you have never been to Nashville, you may think that the temple is a movie set. It is not. In 1897, the Tennessee Centennial and International Exhibition was mounted in celebration of the one hundredth anniversary of Tennessee's admission to the Union as the sixteenth state. At the close of the exhibition, the site was renamed Centennial Park and the exhibition's buildings and exhibits were torn down, save one—a full-size plaster replica of the Parthenon, put up in recognition of Nashville's reputation as the Athens of the South. Plaster doesn't last long in Nashville's humid climate, so in the 1920s, the city fathers pulled down the plaster replica and replaced it with another, this one made of reinforced concrete and meant to last forever.

After sending us on one lap around the columned portico to make sure that all our energy was sapped, Nanny would take us into the dim and hushed interior of the Parthenon. We would start with the smaller of its two rooms. This was paradise for me. Ranged around the walls of this chamber were plaster casts of the ruined statuary that once graced the pediment of the original temple in Athens. Each god or group of gods was identified with a small label affixed to the cement block on which it rested. I was mystified by the ability of any scholar to identify who was who among these gods, since none of the statues had heads and few had any identifying attributes other than the gauzy drapery that they wore. Some did not even have that. I was, of course, particularly drawn to the headless and clothingless statues of the male gods and did not regret too much that most of them were also penis-less since the ones who weren't were so modestly endowed anyway. I always headed first for the statue of Hercules, not only to admire his muscles (and mourn the loss of his feet, hands and penis) but also because Hercules was an occasional guest star in *Thor* comic books. I loved Greek myths as much as I loved comic books. I knew them all. My favorites involved Hermes (penis-less in the Parthenon, also headless, armless, and legless). Among the goddesses, my favorites were Athena and Artemis, who were the most like boys. I felt a particular affinity with Athena, figuring her position as goddess of wisdom on Mt. Olympus was something like my own as champion of the honor roll at school. Like the other goddesses in the Parthenon, Athena had no head, arms, or legs, and the one breast that showed through the flimsy cloth of her drapery seemed puny by Hollywood standards.

After exploring the statues in the smaller chamber, we would walk into the large one. This chamber was empty, save for a hollow wooden post in the center of the room. This post was about five feet tall and was topped with a small bronze statuette of Athena, here with all her limbs intact, her head helmeted, and her chest covered by an armored breastplate. On the post below Athena were a coin-sized slot and a sign encouraging the onlooker to make a deposit toward Nashville's goal of replacing this tiny statuette with a full-scale, forty-foot-tall recreation of the statue that adorned the original Parthenon in Greece. I had seen the movie *Attack of the 50-Foot Woman* on television. Athena would be ten feet shorter, not quite large enough to pick up a car with her bare hands. However, where in the movie Nancy Archer had stomped around town in her underwear, Athena would stand regally in full armor. She would hold a spear in one hand and the winged goddess Nike in the other. At her feet would be coiled a giant serpent. Her shield would be twelve feet across. It seemed like a bargain to me. I would stand there in the gloom, transfixed by the vision of a forty-foot Athena, and wait until Nanny herded the other kids out the door and onto the portico. Then, while they stood blinking in the sunlight, I would quickly empty my pockets of all the money I had. One by one I would push the coins into the slot, wondering how many years would pass before I could stand in that spot and gaze up at the full forty-foot glory of the goddess who sprang full-grown from the forehead of Zeus.

In the two years I attended McGavock, Kent Cathcart mounted several productions in the fully equipped 576-seat theater, including *Our Town* and *Doctor Faustus*. But our main-stage offerings were only sideshows to the circus that was happening elsewhere. The center ring, quite literally, was in classroom S-01.

Kent was hired before the building was even finished and was given carte blanche to outfit his classroom any way he wished. That offer resulted in a classroom unlike any I had ever seen. In the center of the gold-carpeted floor of S-01 was what was known in the decorating magazines of the 1970s as a conversation pit. This was a circular flat-bottomed bowl sunk about eighteen inches into the middle of the room. Between the floor of the classroom and the floor of the bowl ran a single carpeted ledge that served as seating. One side of the bowl was blunted by the suggestion of a stage that thrust out a few feet into the circle. Behind the stage was a curved wall and behind that, a shallow backstage area. In one corner of the room was a small booth with controls for the theatrical lights that hung from the ceiling. S-01 had no desks, chairs or other furniture of any kind. The room was empty until the students arrived.

On the first day of class, Kent passed around copies of *Webster's Dictionary*. They were perfectly ordinary dictionaries except for one detail: the word "coincidence" was missing. Kent had whited it out of every copy.

To some degree, this book is just another retelling of the classic story of a provincial boy whose eyes are opened to the wide world outside his home when he meets his great teacher. Many people, maybe most, hopefully all, have had such a person in their lives. In this story, the shoes of the great teacher are filled by a theater director, academic and mystic named Kent Cathcart. What I was never able to figure out in the years I lay sprawled on the carpet at the feet of my great teacher was just what twist of fate could be powerful enough to send a man of such learning and wisdom into a Nashville classroom and a job as a high school teacher. It was not until many years later, in a long and very expensive phone call from my apartment in New York to his in Nashville, that Kent told me the story of his life. Greatly abridged, it goes as follows:

Like most of his students, Kent started out life as a Southern Baptist. Like us, he took an early interest in theater. Kent was an only child and his parents hoped he would attend Vanderbilt University and stay in Nashville. But by the time he graduated from high school, Kent had already performed in every theatrical venue in town. Kent wanted to go to New York. He applied to Columbia and from there moved on to the graduate theater program at the University of Iowa. It was then that he had his first mystical experience. Driven half-mad by a woman, he got into his car one day and started driving. He had no destination in mind and just kept driving until he could drive no farther. At the California coast, he parked his car by the beach, watched the Pacific Ocean, then got into his car an hour later and drove back to Iowa. Late that night, in the middle of nowhere, Kent heard a voice. The voice very clearly told him that he would become a Catholic. Tired and hungry, Kent stopped early that morning at the first Catholic church he found. He was just in time for prayers. Afterward, a kindly priest gave him breakfast and a prayer book. From that time on, Kent began every day by reciting the prayers of the divine office. He married a Catholic girl and took her to Los Angeles, where they became lay missionaries. Kent supported his growing family by teaching at the University of Southern California while working on his doctorate. By that time the swinging '60s were in full, kaleidoscopic swing. Kent and his wife made new friends, among them people who were famous or soon-to-be famous, like Christopher Isherwood, Anais Nin, and Carlos Castaneda. They talked late into the night with their friends about expanded consciousness and how to get it, most particularly through Vedanta mysticism, psychoanalysis, and hallucinogenic drugs. Kent experimented with new ideas. His wife experimented with substances. Their marriage ended in divorce when Kent's wife became addicted to drugs.

Kent's next move was to commit academic suicide. He had just gotten custody of his two young daughters. As a newly single parent, he realized that his life would be unmanageable unless he was on the same school schedule as his children. Kent left the doctoral program at USC and said good-bye to Los Angeles and to any hopes he had of academic success. Back in Nashville, he had been offered the opportunity to design his own theater in a new state-of-the-art high school and to run it any way he wished. The academic theater director immediately grasped that what looked like academic exile could also be seen as a golden opportunity. Like other progressive theater artists, Kent had studied the theories of the avant-garde theater directors whose companies sprang up around the world in the 1960s. With his own theater, Kent would be able to turn theatrical theory into theatrical experiment and from there, into actual cutting-edge production. The only catch was that he would have to do it with high school students—in Nashville, Tennessee, the Buckle of the Bible Belt.

One day my cousin Rick dropped the needle onto a new record album he said I just had to hear. Three guitar chords later, the war cry "I'm an alligator!" soared up into the beamed ceiling of my parents' family room. My moonage daydream had begun.

If David Bowie has accepted Jesus Christ as his personal Lord and Savior, he will go to heaven when he dies. I hope he has. I hope he does. I can't wait to see what he will wear.

God knows he wore whatever he felt like on earth in the early seventies. Who could ever forget the sight of David Bowie and Marianne Faithfull on late-night TV singing "I've Got You, Babe," she in a nun's habit and he in six-inch pumps and pink latex hot pants, his torso covered only by a fan of showgirl plumes? I had no such finery to wear to the Bowie concert that was announced not long after. Kim, Rick and I bought tickets for the best seats we could afford and then started planning our outfits. Rick picked out a skintight cream-colored pullover embroidered on the chest with a large green-and-orange dragon. His shoulder-length flaxen hair was hard to see against the cream-colored shirt, so he paired it with his other favorite thing, a brown corduroy sport coat with red plaid elbow and shoulder patches. I settled on a skintight white pullover because it looked sensational with my three-inch black suede platform shoes and my lime-green drive-in-movie pants (zippers from the waistband all the way down the front of both legs to the ankles—think about it). Kim went for her usual earth-hippie look, which was a peasant blouse, a fringed shawl, turquoise jewelry, and McGavock High's most elaborately patched, beaded and embroidered bell-bottom blue jeans, many features of which couldn't be seen at all because her blonde hair was so long she could sit on it. On the night of the concert, Rick and I waited impatiently in her bedroom while Kim painted her eyelashes blue; then I drove us downtown to the War Memorial Auditorium.

Since no rock concert ever started on time, we had time to look around as the other members of the audience wandered, floated, rushed, or staggered in, depending on what they had smoked or swallowed in the parking lot. I have never enjoyed being in a crowd of people as much as I did being at a rock concert in the 1960s. Technically this was not the 1960s; it was 1973, but the era that we call the sixties didn't really get started until about the middle of that decade and it did not reach the full flower of its baroque period until the 1970s. By that time, everybody was so liberated in his or her self-expression that any farm boy who showed up to see David Bowie that night stood out from the crowd of hippies as a marvel of individuality. Broadly speaking, there were three types of gorgeous on display that night. The back-to-the-land movement was very popular in the home of country music, so the largest group of people by far at any concert was the earth hippies. These were people who showed up to see David Bowie because, hey, it was a rock concert, after all, but they would have preferred to see the Allman Brothers or Neil Young. The men among them favored tie-dyed T-shirts or plaid flannel button-downs with sleeves rolled up to reveal thermal underwear beneath. Their girlfriends were dressed like my sister. Less numerous but more visible than the earth hippies were the gender-benders, who, whether male or female, mimicked the elaborate makeup and macabre costumes of Alice Cooper or the space alien platform-shoed glitz of David Bowie. I had set out to be a part of that second group but, after looking around, realized that I would never be daring enough to leave the house showing that much skin set off by that much glitter. The third type of gorgeous there that night was the squares, who had not yet worn their parents down to the point of getting to grow their hair long or wear jeans that would fall apart without patches. They were gorgeous just because they looked so different from everyone else.

We were long past any hope of getting home by our curfew when the Spiders from Mars struck the opening chords to "Suffragette City." Moments later, Bowie himself strode on to the stage in a pair of impossibly high platform shoes. I felt pressure in my chest. There he was, only a dozen rows away, David Bowie, my idol, right there in front of me, at that very moment—and the next moment and the next. Four songs into the set, the pressure in my chest was still there. I felt like I wanted to run, and I felt like I never wanted to leave. Something was happening to me. I didn't know what it was, but I knew it had something to do with Bowie, something to do with the vistas that opened up in my head when I heard all the references to outer space in his lyrics; with the potentials just out of reach of consciousness that were conjured up by his glittering, androgynous costumes; with the fear excited by the pale skin those costumes revealed; and with the beauty of his face surrounded by its nimbus of bright red hair. Only once in my life had I had that feeling of exhilaration and fear that only happens when it seems that your fate itself depends on the action that you take in that moment. I had felt it powerfully when I prayed to Jesus to save my soul. Now I had the sense that once again I was being offered the promise of a richer, more rewarding life and that I would have to choose, maybe sooner than later, whether or not to accept it.

I had begun to fear that Bowie would not sing my favorite song when at last I heard the three familiar chords that announced "Moonage Daydream." The pressure in my chest swelled as I waited for the lyrics that had hung in my mind like forbidden fruit since the first time I heard them:

> Don't fake it, baby,
> Lay the real thing on me.
> The church of man, love,
> Is such a holy place to be.

The church of man did not exist as far as I knew, but looking around at all the beautiful people there that night, each dressed to his or her unique best, and at the celebrant on stage whose presence promised a world free of all expectation and constraint, I had an idea of what such a church might be. It did seem like something that could be called holy, and if I understood David Bowie's meaning aright, I was already a member.

The house was dark when we got home. I turned off the ignition at the top of the driveway and coasted the car to a stop in the parking area next to my parents' bedroom. We snuck in through the front door and tiptoed through the quiet house to the far end where the children's bedrooms were. Kim and Rick were sleepy and content. I was hopelessly, head-over-platformed-heels in love.

I had been to rock concerts before—plenty of them, in fact. Like all the kids my age, I had resolved to see every single rock band that came to Nashville. That meant getting a job. My parents kept my allowance deliberately small so that I would have to earn something for myself and, they hoped, learn the value of a dollar. That put me in a tough spot. On the one hand, I needed to work so I could buy tickets to concerts and put gas in the car. On the other hand, the champion of the honor roll needed time to study and time as well to attend rehearsals for all the plays Kent was planning. The solution to this problem came from Rick's friend Norma Jean, a charmingly awkward girl who lived down the street from Nanny. Norma Jean knew the value of a dollar and had three jobs at least, one of which was working the concession stand at the Municipal Auditorium. She told me that I could get a job there as an usher. Not only would I see every show for free, but I would not have to work every night. When there was a show in town, the head usher would call, and if I wasn't available, he would just go to the next person on his list. It was a dream job for a high school student who couldn't hold down a regular work schedule.

As an usher, I saw every rock act that came to Nashville and never paid unless the band booked another venue, which they usually didn't because the Municipal Auditorium was the largest one in town. Sometimes I was stationed where I could see not only the stage but back into the wings, where the performers were preparing to go on—Mick Jagger, limbering up, and Liza Minnelli, frantically stabbing out a cigarette before taking the stage to sing and dance for a solid hour.

Best of all was the Gospel Music Convention. Just Us had disbanded, but I still loved gospel music. The Gospel Music Convention was the only event outside of Holiday on Ice that lasted a whole week, so I made a lot of money. The show began every night with the wife of Reverend Snow playing the organ on stage. Reverend Snow had an octagonal evangelical temple on Dickerson Road. It was the first nondenominational church I had ever seen and it therefore looked very suspect to me. Reverend Snow's wife wore long, splashy gowns and had platinum blonde hair teased up high on top and then tumbling in soft waves down to her waist, in the style of Loretta Lynn. Reverend Snow's wife also looked very suspect to me. She was too flashy by a magnitude of ten to be a preacher's wife. In fact, all the female gospel singers wore floor-length gowns and had long, tumbling hair. I had seen many of them on stage before. What I had not seen were women of the audience decked out in similar style. I had never seen ordinary women dressed like that except in their prom pictures. I was convinced they were prostitutes.

I had never seen a prostitute but felt pretty sure that if one showed up at the Gospel Music Convention, she would do her best to look like a country music star. "I'll bet that's one," I would say to myself as I walked around the concourse during intermissions. The ultimate moment of judging books by their covers came when, standing at my station in the mezzanine, I spotted two women in floor-length black gowns, one redheaded and the other blonde, scurrying across the floor below on their way to their seats. It was Friday night, and nobody had worn black all week. "Now those two for sure," I said. Imagine my horror when I snuck downstairs an hour later to get a closer look at the performers and happened to spy the two women of the night seated in the third row. It was my mother! And her best friend, Betty! They had raided the closet of Betty's daughter and fetched out Donna's two black prom dresses—who wears black to the prom?—junior *and* senior year! I knew my mother had never been to one of these conventions but evidently Betty had, and she knew just how to dress. I was mortified! What could I do but turn it over to Jesus? I asked him to forgive me for judging people. Then, just in case, I prayed that if any of those other women who were not my righteous mother and her best friend did happen to be prostitutes, he would forgive them, too. I am sure Jesus forgave all the prostitutes in the room, if he found any.

The first stage show Kent put on that year at McGavock was *Our Town*. I played the professor who, in the first act, delivers the history of the area where the play is set. Professor Willard declares the land under Grover's Corners to be some of the oldest in the world. Hundreds of millions of years had gone into the making of the imaginary town where every night for a week, Sherry Knott playing Rebecca Gibbs sat atop a ladder representing a second-floor bedroom and marveled at a letter delivered by the postman, even though the address on the envelope was Crofut Farm, Grover's Corners, Sutton

County, New Hampshire, United States of America, continent of North America, Western Hemisphere, the Earth, the solar system, the universe, the mind of God.

Professor Willard had nothing to do in the second act. At the top of the third, as Lyle Gregory playing the stage manager set the somber mood, I took my place in a row of chairs meant to represent the graves of Grover's Corners' deceased. A forty-foot-wide projection of the night sky, looking toward the Milky Way, filled the flat white wall at the back of the stage. Each night Professor Willard stared straight ahead and listened as Julie Seitzman playing Emily Webb bid good-bye to Grover's Corners and clocks ticking and coffee and sunflowers as she realized that the earth she had just left was too wonderful for the living to realize, and Barnetta Carter playing Mrs. Webb quietly agreed that the living just don't understand, and the starlight shining from the center of the galaxy finished its million-year journey to the stage of the theater at McGavock Comprehensive High School.

2900 Rich Acres Drive, Nashville, Davidson County, Tennessee, United States of America, North American continent, planet Earth, solar system, Milky Way galaxy, the universe, the mind of God, where everything happens *now*. How long does it take starlight to travel from one end of the universe to the other?

How long does it take starlight to travel from one end of God's mind to the other? Does it travel at the speed of light or at the speed of thought? If it travels at the speed of thought, does it arrive the moment it leaves? Can it then be said to have arrived at all? Or to have left? Scientists tell us that two atomic particles, having once interacted, will always be aware of each other, even if they end up on opposite sides of the universe. Is this because they have formed some special bond by interacting? Or is it because they never went anywhere, is it because there is nowhere else to go in the mind of God where leaving happens the moment you arrive?

"One thought fills immensity."—*William Blake.*

Halfway through my junior year, I was standing in a knot of kids outside the door to S-01 when I felt a poke in the ribs. Turning around, I looked into a pair of languid green eyes, level with my own. The eyes belonged to another student in Kent's class, a senior named Suzanne. Suzanne was one of the Prickly Heat Sisters, a loose confederation of earth hippies who pretended to fondle their own and each other's breasts in public and who shared a fervent belief in the redeeming power of Elton John. I never knew precisely how many Prickly Heat Sisters there were but could easily count a dozen, several of whom, like Sherry and Suzanne, were in Kent's class.

The Prickly Heat Sisters were beautiful, intelligent, and fun, which was why it did not occur to me at first that one of them might want to be my girlfriend. Barnetta and Beth soon fixed that, cornering me a week later to explain the birds and the bees, Beth beginning her explanation with an indignant "Michael!" and Barnetta beginning hers with "You idiot!" Once I understood what was happening, I was happy to play along. I liked Suzanne. I even thought I was attracted to her. Soon, I was in a pickle.

The prom was coming up. I had not worked long as an usher and had not saved enough money to purchase prom tickets, rent a tuxedo, buy a corsage, and pay for dinner for two at the Jolly Ox Steakhouse. I proposed instead that Suzanne and I go to the movies that night and meet up with our friends later for dinner. Everybody thought proms were corny and Suzanne seemed perfectly happy to skip it. Imagine my surprise, then, when I showed up at her door and she answered it wearing a ball gown. I thought it was so that she would not look out of place with the other girls at dinner. It was not until many years later that I realized that Suzanne thought I was joking about the movies and that she fully expected to be whisked off to the prom at the last minute. I hope she has forgiven me for being such a dolt. St. Clare of Assisi would have, as would have St. Francis, also of Assisi and the subject of the movie I took Suzanne to see.

Suzanne enjoyed *Brother Sun, Sister Moon*, or was kind enough to say she did. I thought it was the greatest movie ever. I loved the way the rich brocades of the clothing were set off by the rough stone of the buildings. I loved the "brother love" that St. Francis's handsome friends sang about after they abandoned their worldly possessions and their prom dates and went out to beg in the streets of Assisi. I loved St. Francis's bowl haircut, his black eyes and his full lips. I wanted to be St. Francis. I wanted to sit in a meadow the livelong day, gazing at flowers and butterflies while arranging the folds of my gorgeous medieval outfits just so. I wanted to look directly into the camera and tell my parents that I only needed a few berries and a few sips of water each day, like the birds of the air. I wanted to watch Pope Alec Guinness stagger down two flights of stairs just to kiss my dirty feet and tell me how holy I was. How could I not love a movie in which the star announces his sainthood by stripping off all his clothes so he can parade butt naked from one end of Assisi to the other while the orchestra informs the crowd that they are witnessing a blessed miracle? That movie solved all my problems for a good six months.

My problem was this: like any teenager, I needed an identity, or failing that, a pose, that would set me apart from the herd just enough to make me unique without setting me apart so much as to make me weird. I arrived at McGavock just a few months after Just Us broke up, so for the first several months of my junior year, I traded on my recent past as a gospel singer and let it be known that the other kids should think of me as a Very Religious Boy. By Easter, the flaw with that identity was obvious: my hair was too short. Being a young Christian could actually be very cool but only if you were a particular kind of young Christian called a Jesus freak. A Jesus freak was a hippie with a Bible instead of a bong. St. Francis's admonition to live life simply, as he hurled his wealthy father's merchandise out the window and into the street, was perfectly in tune with the hippie sensibility of the early 1970s. So was his teaching that we should love all creatures. St. Francis would have been a perfect Jesus freak, if his hair had just been three inches longer. I resolved to morph from a good Christian boy into a Jesus freak. I would grow my hair long, pray more, and love simple but tasteful things, like St. Francis.

My parents had always been more stylish than my friends' parents, and my father had grown his hair halfway over his ears, like Burt Reynolds, for whom Dad was mistaken on more than one occasion despite the fact that Dad lived in Nashville and Burt Reynolds did not. I was allowed to wear my hair as long as my father wore his and no longer, until I pointed out that Burt at church and lately of Just Us had a sensational haircut that completely covered his ears. My parents agreed that Burt did indeed look very nice and they allowed me to grow my hair long enough to get that same haircut. What a mess! My hair was thick and wavy and stuck out in every direction while Burt's was sleek as an otter's pelt, but the important thing was that my baseline haircut was now long enough to cover my ears! My good fortune was compounded when I landed a summer job as an intern at Jenny Wiley Theater, an outdoor theater in Jenny Wiley State Park in Prestonsburg, Kentucky. I would be in good company there; Lyle Gregory, a clean-cut lad who had sung

with Just Us and would go on in his senior year to become
Tennessee State Teenager of the Year or something like that,
got an internship as well. My parents figured that a couple
of wholesome Christians like Lyle and me could be counted
on to keep each other out of trouble, so they agreed to let
me spend the whole summer away. With three months of no
parental supervision and a salary of only twenty-five dollars
a week that would not allow for visits to the barber shop, I
could let my hair grow all summer long.

It did not take long to figure out that Lyle had other plans
for his summer besides walking the straight and narrow. I
was left to battle Satan by myself. Every Sunday morning in
Prestonsburg, I got up and went to church while the rest of
the summer stock company slept off their hangovers. I even
followed St. Francis's lead to the extent of visiting the local
Catholic church, but when no art-directed epiphany occurred
to me there like the one St. Francis had in the ruined chapel
of San Damiano, I admitted to myself that I preferred Baptist
hymns and went back to a Baptist church I had discovered
on my first day in town. Every week, my hair inched closer
to the length I needed for the new identity I had picked out
for my senior year of high school. By the time my parents
came to see me perform in *Damn Yankees*, I had been on my
own long enough to earn the right to wear my hair as long
as I wanted. I was well on my way to becoming a Jesus freak.

Then, on my last night in Prestonsburg, after my bags were
packed and my room in the old hotel where the company
lived was swept clean, Satan tricked me into taking a toke

off a joint that someone offered me by saying that I should at least know what it tasted like. He then suggested the same about wine, beer, vodka and Quaaludes. My new friends in the cast and crew were celebrating their last night together by pooling their pot, drugs and booze for one last blowout party before leaving town the next day and I wanted to celebrate with them, knowing how much I would miss them all. All I remember about that party is a toilet I befriended when my stomach rebelled at all the unaccustomed stuff I had poured into it. When at last I finished throwing up, I climbed out a window, reeled across the roof of the porch and collapsed on an old mattress that someone had dragged out there weeks before. I was shivering in the early morning damp when I woke just enough to see a hazy figure spreading a blanket over me. It was probably one of the older techies of the company, but in my foggy state of mind I thought that the bearded, long-haired man was Jesus. I thanked him and went back to sleep.

A week later I walked back into McGavock High School with my hair longer than it had ever been and no interest at all in being a Jesus freak. That was okay. Soon, I had another and better identity in mind.

In 1968, the year that *Hair* moved to Broadway, Jerzy Grotowski wrote a book called *Towards a Poor Theatre*. Grotowski was director of the Polish Laboratory Theatre, which was at that time the most highly regarded experimental theater in the world. Shortly after my senior year began, Kent read a short passage from the book to his fourth-period advanced drama class:

> Theatre—through the actor's technique, his art in which the living organism strives for higher motives—provides an opportunity for what could be called integration, the discarding of masks, the revealing of the real substance: a totality of physical and mental reactions. This opportunity must be treated in a disciplined manner, with a full awareness of the responsibilities it involves. Here we can see the theatre's therapeutic function for people in our present day civilization. It is true that the actor accomplishes this act, but he can only do so through an encounter with the spectator—intimately, visibly, not hiding behind a cameraman, wardrobe mistress, stage designer or make-up girl—in direct confrontation with him, and somehow "instead of" him. The actor's act—discarding half measures, revealing, opening up, emerging from himself as opposed to closing up—is an invitation to the spectator. This act could be compared to an act of the most deeply rooted, genuine love between two human beings—this is just a comparison since we can only refer to this "emergence from oneself" through analogy. This act, paradoxical and borderline, we call a total act. In our opinion it epitomizes the actor's deepest calling.

That was the theater that Kent Cathcart came to McGavock High School to teach. Seen through the lens of history, that paragraph serves up, in one bite, the entire smorgasbord of

ideas that nourished the artistic, social and political rebel-
lions of the time. Note especially the words "encounter" and
"therapeutic." McGavock Comprehensive High School was
founded in the heyday of the encounter group, the happening, the be-in, and the commune. It was also the heyday of
the back-to-the-land movement. All these movements were
variations on a theme of authenticity, of the idea that people
could set aside the masks of social convention and engage
each other—and themselves—without artifice. For the theater,
this meant doing away with the proscenium arch. For the
performer, it meant doing away with the role. In a laboratory
of experimental theater, the performer did not just portray
a character in a play. In a laboratory theater, the performer
revealed his essential self. What that meant in practice was that
experimental theater often looked as much like psychotherapy
as it did performance.

After class, I asked Kent if I could see the book. Flipping
through *Towards a Poor Theatre* in the few minutes I had
before my next class, I came upon some photographs of a lean
young actor playing the title role in Grotowski's production
of *The Constant Prince*. He was naked, save for a loincloth.
Ryszard Cieslak's body was distorted by the pain inflicted by
his persecutors, while his face was illuminated by a faraway
look somewhere between suffering, ecstasy, and grace. I had
seen many pictures like this, usually on Sunday. Here were images of a theater that went far beyond psychotherapy. Looking
at the pictures of Cieslak, I thought again of the paragraph
Kent had read aloud and of some of the phrases it contained:

"full awareness," "genuine love," "total act," "deepest calling." Ryszard Cieslak had short hair. Except for that, he looked like nothing so much as Christ.

Kent's subject the following week was humanistic psychology. He made sure to sit under the brightest spotlight in the room as he described Abraham Maslow's concept of self-actualization, that human need to manifest our full potential once our basic needs for safety and sustenance are met. The idea of self-actualization was like an aphrodisiac for a classroom of bright kids who were struggling to find and express their unique identities. Even after Kent explained it, I had only the vaguest notion of what self-actualization was, but whatever it was, I wanted it. Whenever I tried to imagine what a self-actualized person looked like, the image that came to mind was Ryszard Cieslak as the Constant Prince. The grainy black-and-white photographs in *Towards a Poor Theatre* showed a man who seemed to have actualized every atom of his being in the service of his art and who in every gesture revealed his essence. "People are hungry for the truth, and we give them truth," Kent said. Theater, it turned out, was not the land of make-believe I had thought it was. I had come to McGavock for theater and had stumbled instead into the high temple of truth. I felt like I had just discovered buried treasure in my backyard. An art form that was the embodiment of truth was something to which I could give my heart and soul. If

I dedicated myself to the theater of truth, if I worked hard enough and sacrificed everything for it, I might even become self-actualized. I might become like Ryszard Cieslak, who was not just an actor but a saint, not just an artist but a holy man.

I had always been called Mike. One day I noticed that Barnetta and Beth were calling me Michael. I thought it was just one of those things that girls do to annoy boys so I ignored them. Much more interesting to me than my name was my hair. I discovered that if I scrunched my neck in back, it was now long enough to brush my shoulders. I started walking around school with my neck scrunched and my hair parted in the middle like a hippie.

I also figured out what to do about the fact that I was undeniably attracted to men and that there was nothing I could do about it. I had given up all hope of being straight, but I was still not willing to admit to myself that I was gay. I decided instead that I would sidestep the question altogether by being celibate. I would be a celibate, artistic holy man, like the Constant Prince.

A week before senior year began, the Rolling Stones single "Angie" was released in the United States. I was crazy about it. I got even crazier when I learned that the Angie of the title was none other than David Bowie's wife, Angela. I went crazier still when I heard about Bowie's alleged response to the song. Asked by the press why Mick Jagger would write a love song about his wife, Bowie is reported to have said, "Because he couldn't very well write one about me."

David Bowie's claim to be bisexual first appeared in print in 1972. Shortly after "Angie" became my new favorite song, I decided that what was good enough for Bowie was good enough for me. Standing in my bedroom one night, staring at Bowie's picture on the cover of his new album *Aladdin Sane,* I added another twist to the sexual self-image that I was cobbling together for myself. I decided to convince myself that I was bisexual. I would be bisexual, like David Bowie. I would be celibate, like the Constant Prince. Bisexual and celibate. I could live with that. I even admired myself for the qualities of tolerance and stoicism that such a compromise required and that I tried to believe I possessed.

"Process is as important as product" was one of Kent's favorite sayings. In S-01, our process consisted of exercises that were meant to rid us of our inhibitions onstage and put us more in touch with our bodies and in tune with each other. Here is a list of theatrical exercises that I still remember from S-01:

Power Spot. This exercise was taken from the writings of Carlos Castaneda. It was an experiment in developing awareness that was not centered in the mind. One day Kent began the class by asking us to walk slowly around the room until we found a spot that felt powerful for us. We were then to claim that spot for the day. The Castaneda fans—a tall marble-skinned mime named Jason Litchford and his best friend, a demonic magician named Steve Burton—went right to work. Within a week the exercise was second nature to all of us. No student in fourth-period advanced drama would ever think of starting class without first finding his power spot. Before long it appeared to me that my friend Beth's power spot was moving closer and closer each day to the power spot of the powerfully built Steve. I had known Beth for years by then and knew that it was only a matter of time before the magician fell under the spell of the aquiline, glacier-eyed beauty inching toward him. By Columbus Day, the two power spots were one.

Mind Trip. This was the exercise Kent led us through when we were having a bad day and threatening to disrupt his sanity. A bad day was when another teacher told us that we were not as special as we thought we were. Kent would dim the lights and have us lie on our power spot. He then described, in great detail, a trip that we would take to another place that left us calmer and quieter than we had been when we burst into the room. Mind trips were sometimes mapped out in advance, but usually Kent made them up on the spot. Dealing with two dozen high-spirited teenagers in a free-form environment every day meant that Kent had to invent a lot of things on the spot, particularly since his fourth-period advanced drama class followed advanced placement English. AP English was taught by Kent's boss and nemesis, the caustic and egg-domed chief of the English department, Dr. James Currey. Dr. Currey's class met around a square table in a small seminar room. On one side of the table sat the bespectacled and cheerful math geniuses, who had written a percussion piece called *Concerto for Briefcase and Book,* which they would play for us until class began. On the other side sat a selection of the Prickly Heat Sisters. Arrayed between them, at the end of the table in Dr. Currey's crosshairs, were the drama students, also known as the "drama queers": me, Barnetta, Beth, Chris Wilson (our soft-spoken and gentle lighting designer), and Gerald Hyland, a slight boy whose outsized talent made him the star of the drama department and whose flamboyance would have been the death of him had there not been something saintly about his tread as he walked the halls—a way he had of walking with his head held perfectly level so that the air caught under the soft wings of his hair and lifted it around his head, making him look as though he were flying. Dr. Currey may have been fond of the eccentric theater kids in his class, but the disdain with which he treated us made it hard to know for sure. He was careful to insinuate at least once a week that creativity proffered no real advantage in the world outside those walls and that he fully expected to see each of us in the newspaper one day, photographed on the way to prison or engaged to marry some perfectly

THE THOUSAND-PETALED LOTUS

ordinary human in preparation for a perfectly ordinary life. He once tried to insult me by calling me a dilettante, thinking I would not know what he meant. I just smiled and thanked him for the compliment, figuring that it was better to know a little about a lot of things than to know a little about nothing at all.

Mirroring. Another classic. Two students would face each other and look intently into each other's eyes. One would slowly move and the other would mirror those movements as exactly as possible. This is the exercise that was made famous by Lucille Ball and Harpo Marx. For this one I would try to pair up with Jason, whose crisp movements were worthy of study, or Ricky Santry just because he was so cute. There were other students I would try to avoid unless I was feeling adventurous. The most difficult to keep up with was Steven Welch, who vied with Gerald for position as the most flamboyant person in the room. Steven was gamine, with a Prince Valiant haircut that he had self-inflicted one afternoon instead of redecorating or doing his homework. Imagine Audrey Hepburn as a man on speed in a ragged medieval haircut. The haircut may have been an impulse decision with blunt scissors, but it was not a mistake. Steven was the bravest person I had ever known. He arrived on the first day of school sporting a leather shoulder bag—"All the best men in New York have them!"—which was promptly snatched from his shoulder and kicked across the room by the sort of boy we referred to in drama class as a "yard ape." Steven ditched the bag but not his right to free speech. In this he was buoyed by the zeitgeist, which placed a premium on individual expression. No one at McGavock High School expressed his individuality as loudly, continually, and creatively as Steven. He was impossible to ignore and impossible to mirror.

Auras. Another exercise lifted straight from the books of Carlos Castaneda. A student would be asked to stand under a spotlight on the stage. The rest of us would squint at her the way that Castaneda's teacher, the shaman Don Juan, taught him to do. By squinting at someone standing in a pool of light, it was possible to discern that person's aura. Soon we were seeing colors, striations, and other anomalies. Soon after that, the exercise devolved into a "Who has the biggest aura?" contest. We stopped doing it after Steve Burton's Lord-of-the-Dark-Arts aura crowded out all the competition.

Trust. An old standard from the world of psychology. A student would stand at the edge of the stage and fall backward, trusting that Barnetta would stop teasing the other kids long enough for them to link hands and catch him before he hit the floor. Trust was important not only to our performances together but to our social lives as well—the words "social lives" here understood to be a euphemism for "peccadilloes" of which there were many, the most notorious of which was a luncheon Barnetta organized at a downtown restaurant called the Gerst Haus. There was no way we could go downtown for lunch without cutting a couple of classes, one of which was advanced placement English.

Imaginary Life Path. Another classic from the world of psychotherapy. The student is asked to lie on his power spot and imagine himself somewhere in the world of nature. He sees a path before him—what kind of path is it? Walking along the path, he finds something—what does he find? What does he do with it? An animal crosses the path—what kind of animal is it? A body of water is encountered—what sort of water is it? How does he cross it? After the imaginary journey was over, Kent told us the psychological meaning of each feature of the path. The object found on the path is opportunity. The animal is the shadow self. For me, those were a key that I put into my pocket and a bear that I shook hands with. So far, so good. Then I was mortified to hear that the body of water represented sexuality. Walking down my woodland path, I had come to a shallow stream about a foot wide, which I hopped across. When I heard that, I decided not to tell the other kids about my imaginary life path. When Barnetta pestered me about it in the car on our way home from school, I arched an eyebrow and told her that it was much too deep to discuss.

Birth. An exercise that we did only once. One student was chosen to be born. Steven Welch elbowed his way to the front of the pack, insisting on some flaw or other with his first birth ("Well, just look at me!") that made a second birth essential. All the other students joined hands, arms, and legs to form a human birth canal, into which Steven wriggled and writhed until he emerged at the far end as a better person.

Metaphor Dance. Another exercise that we did only once. Once was enough for me. Waiting for my turn, I felt like I was going to the guillotine. Sitting on the edge of the stage, Kent asked each student in turn to leave his or her power spot and move into the center of the circle. The instructions were simple: dance your metaphor. The idea was to move without thought or intention and let the body itself take the form that most expressed the student's inner being. Kent's only other instruction was that we should avoid thinking ahead about what we would do while we were waiting for our turn. That wasn't hard to do since my heart was pounding too hard to think about anything at all. I watched Barnetta extend her fists and bounce as though holding the reins to a runaway bronco that was expending its life as fast as it could. I watched Steven Welch spin around the room and strike himself until he fell to the floor in a heap of self-destructive fury. I watched Gerald kneel and sway with arms outstretched as though praying on a flying carpet. When my turn came, I planted my feet in the center of the circle, lifted my arms above my head, and swayed forward and backward in an undulating movement from my ankles to my fingertips, like an underwater plant swayed by the current.

This list sets forth only a fraction of the exercises that we did in S-01. They were powerful experiences for a boy who had just begun to venture outside the sacred precinct of the Baptist Church. But the exercise that beyond all others fired my imagination and the imaginations of all the children in advanced drama class, the activity that we did day after day and week after week, the one thing that we simply could not get enough of, was improvisation. That most terrifying of theatrical forms was like heroin to performers who were also teenagers and therefore risk-takers from sunup to sundown. Seeing that we responded so readily to improvisation, Kent invented his own form of improvisational theater. He called it formats and scenarios.

The schoolteachers we all remember are the ones who wander off their subjects and teach us about life. Kent's subject was theater, but his teaching often seemed more like channeling as he shared with us what appeared to be an intergalactic perspective on life. Everything Kent said had significance beyond its immediate application. Everything he said was deep. Soon "deep" became the ultimate praise for anything that happened in S-01. Soon, too, Kent acquired the nickname that he would carry for years to come: "Cosmic."

"You are who you know and what you've read." Kent might just as well have added "and the movies you've seen." Up to the moment when I saw *Brother Sun, Sister Moon,* my favorite movie was *Planet of the Apes.* Kent insisted that we see foreign films. He invited Barnetta, Beth, Gerald, and me to his apartment one evening for homemade Asian food and then took us to the Belcourt Theater for a showing of *Ugetsu.* Another night it was Italian food and Fellini's *8½.* I was astonished by the movies. I was just as astonished by Kent's apartment. It was unlike any dwelling I had ever seen. My parents were the only people I knew who did not outfit every room of their house with a matching suite of furniture and a mass-produced painting, but even our tasteful furniture was bought new at a furniture store. Kent had antiques and huge mirrors and a cloud-painted canvas on the ceiling over his bed. He had curiosities and art and art books and shelves of yet more books. Kent was well read and he not only discussed books in class but recommended them to us. If he thought a student had no money to buy a book, Kent would lend it, and if he thought he would never get the book back, he gave it away. Kent was also a consummate name-dropper. We knew who Kent was, not only from hearing about the books he had read but from hearing about the people he knew as well. Some of them, we met ourselves.

I had already met Ruth Sweet at the Body Shop. If Ruth had been born full-grown like Athena, her parents would have known what they had on their hands and named her Lola. Think Lola from *Damn Yankees*, Gwen Verdon singing and dancing to "Whatever Lola Wants, Lola Gets." Ruth was not a Nashville native. She moved there from Boston to run the drama program at Fisk University. Ruth began dropping by S-01 whenever Fisk was in recess. Class was never as exciting as it was on the days when we spilled into the room and found Ruth in her sunglasses sitting on the edge of the circle with Kent. Ruth wore sunglasses all day long and all night too, no matter where she was. One night at a party, she decided that she wanted to dance—with me—and she took her sunglasses off. When Ruth looked at me with her naked eyes, my limbs went limp. Think Lola from the Kinks' 1970 hit single, who walked like a woman and talked like a man. Ruth had the deepest voice of any woman I have ever known. Every word she spoke with it was riveting. "Do something, something happens," she would say, dropping a verbal stone into the pond of my mind that would cause ripples for days. Everything that Kent taught us about theater was embodied by Ruth. She was yin to Kent's yang. Each was like a mirror in which the other's reflection was magnified.

If Ruth was Kent's theatrical consort, his best friend, Douglas Williams, was grand vizier. He was not yet forty when he stepped into our classroom for the first time, but his hair was already white, which made him as striking in his own way as Ruth was in hers. Doug believed heart and soul in the redemptive power of the creative act in any form. As a young man he had been a professional musician. He played marimba on the *Arthur Godfrey Show*, toured South America, and then set himself up as an interior decorator. Doug had never studied interior decoration, but lack of knowledge never stopped Doug from doing anything. For the ladies of Nashville he created tasteful interiors. "All they want is furniture," he would say. For himself, he created wonders out of nothing. To my sheltered eyes, each of his houses was a new world of possibilities for life and how it could be lived more adventurously than had ever been imagined at 2900 Rich Acres Drive. The walls of one house were covered in corrugated tin. The dining table in another had no legs but was suspended by chains from the center of the ceiling where the chandelier should have been. One apartment had no furniture at all, Doug having decided at that time that the ideal dwelling was one that could be hosed down at the end of the day. In 1973, Doug moved into an old house across the street from the Parthenon. It had a small kitchen, with only the most rudimentary cooking equipment, and behind that an even smaller room that was just large enough for a bed. The rest of the house had no rooms at all because Doug had torn out all the interior walls. He painted the open space white and put a sign on the front door of the house that read "Hammelbacher Gallery." I was shocked when Kent told me that the doors of Hammelbacher were never locked unless there were paintings on exhibit. Doug was the first person I ever met who believed that if a person needed something so much that he had to steal it, then he was welcome to have it. The irony of course was that if there was no art on exhibit, there was nothing whatsoever in the house to steal. The only thing of value that Doug had was a marimba that he kept in the attic and that would have been difficult for a thief to roll out of the house unnoticed. Everything else Doug owned was in the trunk of his Lincoln Town Car.

I met plenty of other people through Kent—professors, musicians, journalists, poets, and others—but Ruth and Doug were the people I would come to know. I adored the three of them. Before long, I thought of Kent, Ruth and Doug less as individuals and more as a package, three in one, a secular trinity to match the holy one I worshipped at church.

I had never been around educated people. The only educated people I had ever known were schoolteachers, who stuck to their subjects, and preachers, who every Sunday taught the word of God as set forth in the Bible, every word of which they said was literally true. Never mind that on Monday morning our schoolteachers would upend the literal truth of the Bible with talk of dinosaurs and history. The Southern Baptist Church of the early 1970s may have been evangelical, it may have been fundamentalist, but it was not exactly creationist. Our parents might take us to church where creation in six days was taught on Sunday, but they expected us to pass a test on evolution the following Monday. If I was asked in Sunday school how long it took God to create the world, I would answer, "Six days." If I was asked on Monday morning how long it took our ancestors to climb down from the trees, I would answer, "Millions of years." One belief was a theory and the other was the God-revealed truth, and I was expected to know both and to believe both. Riding home from church one Sunday, I asked my parents just exactly how I was supposed to do this. The answer I got from the front seat was the stock answer the Southern Baptist Church gave everyone: "A thousand years is as a day to God, and a day is as a thousand years." Sitting on the hard wooden pews of Hillhurst Baptist Church Sunday after Sunday as the sermons dragged on, I could see how that might be true.

The day-is-a-thousand-years explanation kept me happy until the following Sunday, when I took time off from ignoring the sermon to examine the first chapter of Genesis more closely. Verses fourteen through nineteen show God setting up his days, seasons, and years by careful arrangement of the sun, moon, and stars. He did this on the fourth day, so presumably on the fifth, sunrise and sunset occurred roughly twelve hours apart. Since God intended to take the seventh day off, that left him only forty-eight hours to finish creation. God spent the fifth day making fish and birds. He started off the sixth day with land animals and finished with the first man. How was it possible for all these things to evolve when sunrise and sunset had already been established? Two possible explanations sprang to mind. The first was that days five and six on planet Earth were not twenty-four hours long because the Almighty Creator made the sun move very, very slowly on those two days. The other explanation was that he sped up evolution so that dinosaurs roamed the earth on the morning of the sixth day but by lunchtime they had turned into saber-toothed tigers and woolly mammoths. Both theories made my head hurt. By the time the sermon was over and we were standing to sing "The Nail-Scarred Hand," I was convinced that creation would have been a lot simpler if, on the third day when God made dry land, he just went ahead and buried dinosaur bones in it along with all the diamonds and minerals and other things that people would dig up later. I never mentioned any of these theories to my science teachers and got an A in science on every report card. I kept them to myself in church as well.

Kent invented formats over lasagna one evening with Ruth and Doug. A format started simply enough. Two students would throw an imaginary ball back and forth. To that motion, one would add a sound, the other the name of a body part, and from those simple elements, an improvisational story would emerge. Nothing was preset; there was no sixty-second planning conference; we had nothing at all to work with when we took our places on the little stage in S-01. The process was terrifying, and everybody wanted to try it. Then everybody wanted to try it again with a different partner. And again. And again. A week later Kent added four actors to the format and called the new form a scenario. Each format and scenario was entirely different from the last. Some were funny, some were poignant, some were surreal. A lot of them were terrible. Many turned psychotherapeutic as teenagers took the opportunity to work out their deepest feelings in a safe environment. Those therapeutic improvs we called "deep."

What we called ourselves was "drama queers." It was the Prickly Heat Sisters among us who first coined the term. The Prickly Heat Sisters were not gay, but then they were not prickly either—if they found a name they liked, they adopted it whether it was accurate or not. The Prickly Heat Sisters were not transfer students like Beth, Barnetta and me. They had lived all their lives among the kids of McGavock High School and they knew exactly what they were dealing with. They knew perfectly well that behind their backs, they were being called queer just for associating with the flamboyant actors of S-01, who could no more blend in with the yahoos at school than a flamingo could troop unnoticed among crows. What the Prickly Heat Sisters did in their collective wisdom was to proclaim themselves "drama queers" in public before anyone else could do it. They were so delighted with their new name that within a week, they had christened every child in S-01 a drama queer, whether that child was gay, straight, or a celibate bisexual. The students of advanced drama were enchanted with our new label. We blithely piled into the big tent of collective identity that the Prickly Heat Sisters had pitched for us and began calling ourselves drama queers everywhere we went. There is strength in numbers. Soon there were so many queers walking the halls of McGavock High that the other students had no idea which queers were real and which were fake. There was no way to single any one of us out, no way to make a victim of any of us. The happy result of the Prickly Heat Sisters' genius was to turn the outrageous students of S-01 into a target that was too big to miss and too big to hit.

"Mike, I have always prayed that someday you would be a preacher." All my life, I had spent at least one weekend night with one of my grandmothers. By senior year, I had too many social activities lined up to do that anymore. One Saturday morning, knowing this might be the last time I would ever wake up in her house, Mama Fields gathered her courage and said what the Lord had laid on her heart. I loved my grandmother too much to trample on her hopes, so I hemmed and hawed about how one never knows how life will turn out. She got the message. I never heard anything about being a preacher again.

How was I supposed to be a preacher when every time I looked at the Bible, I wondered just how it could actually be God's word? In my own bed that night, lying awake as I did most nights, I tested the bars of my spiritual prison, rehearsing doubts that only seemed to multiply. I knew that some centuries had elapsed between the conclusion of the Old Testament and the beginning of the New. Did this mean that God stopped talking between the books of Malachi and Matthew? Did God stop talking altogether when the book of Revelation was finished? Did God have nothing left to say? Was there nothing important enough for God to talk about other than what he said to us when he answered our prayers? Why would God choose to have his words published back then and not now? Was God's reading public never to get a sequel?

It was well past midnight and all hope of getting a good night's sleep was gone when God's plan for salvation presented itself for my review. I fluffed my pillow, straightened the covers, and lay on my back with my hands crossed over my chest like a corpse. The rationale behind the plan was that mankind had strayed so far from righteousness that only the biggest sacrifice imaginable would appease God's wrath. The only sacrifice big enough to do the job was the sacrifice of

God himself. God therefore caused a virgin to conceive and give birth, then traded the life of his child for the salvation of every subsequent human being who accepts Jesus Christ as his personal Lord and Savior. The plan seemed so complicated. Why not just abolish hell altogether? Satan might object, but was he really in a position to say no, once Almighty God decided to send in the bulldozers? If the goal was to rescue mankind from eternal damnation as the price for his sins, why would the Almighty not simply change human nature so that people would stop sinning altogether?

God works in mysterious ways, as every preacher I had ever known was quick to point out. I knew that it was not the place of a Nashville teenager, even one with report cards like mine, to question the will of God. Still, I wondered about his timing as the hands on the alarm clock inched toward three. If the only way to get to heaven was to accept Jesus Christ as your personal Lord and Savior, what happened to all the people who lived and died before Jesus was even born? I knew Moses and Elijah went to heaven because Jesus spoke with them during his transfiguration. But what about Abraham, Isaac, Joseph, and David? What about the rest of God's chosen people? What about everyone else? Why would God wait until AD 0 to send mankind a savior? It did not seem fair. It would have made much more sense, I thought, if Jesus's mother had been Bathsheba. Or Sarah. Or, for that matter, Eve.

It was this kind of thinking, lying awake nights staring into the dark, that led me to wonder whether that little Indian boy, now grown tall and strong on all the leftovers my mother sent him, might make it into heaven after all.

I imagined a boy in India not much different from myself. I thought of the boy's straight-A report cards, his prudishness and his piety. Surely he believed in his gods as strongly as I believed in mine—why wouldn't he? And yet purely by accident of birth, he lived in a place where people had never heard of Jesus Christ and therefore had little alternative but to believe that thousands of gods would be necessary to get a world up and running. Was it the Indian boy's fault that he was going to hell? How could it be that I could go to heaven just because I accepted an opportunity that was pushed at me from every direction where I came from, yet he, who was just as good a child in his land as I was in mine, would go to hell just because Jesus had been born to a Jew and not to a Hindu? If he were as good a child in his world as I was in mine, was it not also possible that his gods were just as good as mine? Was it not also possible that the Hindu heaven and hell were just the same as ours, only with different names? If I asserted that the God I worshipped was the one true God, and if he was a just God, was it not reasonable to assume that he would welcome my Hindu counterpart into heaven the same way he welcomed me?

In those moments of doubt, a liberal humanist worm crept into the Southern Baptist apple. I still went to church every Sunday. But while before I sat through the sermons and doodled, now I sat through the sermons and thought. It occurs to me now that doodling may be more conducive to faith than thought. The more I thought, the more I found to think about. That first consideration of my Hindu friend formed a crack in the smooth, hard surface of my faith. Soon the crack would be a pothole, and soon after that, a crater in the middle of my faith. I still had a savior, but if my Hindu friend was going to join me in heaven, it meant that there must be other ways to be born again than by being washed in the blood of the Lamb.

For weeks we did nothing but formats and scenarios. By December of my senior year, we had become so proficient at improvisation that Kent decided to take his show on the road. He rented a small second-floor space near Vanderbilt University called the Ensemble Theatre Company, or ETC for short. He engaged a printer to make flyers announcing performances to begin two months hence, on March 9. Then Kent Cathcart changed the name of his fourth-period class from advanced drama to Theater of the Mind.

I stopped scrunching my neck. By the end of first semester senior year, my hair was undeniably shoulder-length in back and long enough everywhere else that I had to repeatedly rake my hand through it to get it out of my eyes. Everybody in S-01 was calling me Michael, including Kent.

All the graduate students of education in Nashville wanted to do their student teaching at McGavock. Kent had two student teachers my senior year. The name of the first I do not recall. All she did was sleep. She slept all day. She slept the entire semester. Kent would dim the lights of S-01 in preparation for an exercise and the student teacher would stretch out on the carpet and fall asleep in the darkened room, no doubt dreaming of some other career that was more to her liking.

The second semester, our student teacher was a lanky and engaging philosophy major named Don Swenholt. Don did not know much about theater, but he knew everything about Plato. Kent turned him loose on us, and for an entire week I watched enraptured as the handsome student teacher loped around the classroom teaching Plato. Don started us off with the allegory of the cave and its depressing assertion that the masses of mankind will spend their lives living in the cave of ignorance, in spite of handsome philosophy majors who point the way out into the sunlight of truth. On Wednesday, Don bewitched me with Plato's theory of forms, those eternal, archetypal ideas of things as they first appear in the mind of God before human beings make a hash of them. By Friday, I had to admit that Don had spent his parents' money and his four years at Vanderbilt wisely. I somehow managed not to fall in love when Don wrapped up the week with Plato's assertion that the archetypal forms are present in man's eternal soul, and therefore, true knowledge cannot be acquired by studying but only by recalling the eternal truths that already lie within us. You might imagine how sweet that sounded to someone like me, who had just spent eleven years cramming for tests—to little avail, I might add. My hopes to become class valedictorian had been torpedoed by a gym teacher who didn't understand that just because the champion of the honor roll couldn't catch a baseball with a bucket, that was no reason to give him a "C." I consoled myself with my new awareness that I had within me eternal truths that would assure my happiness someday, if only I could remember them.

Not every book I read was assigned in school. Listening to Don talk about the most famous philosopher who ever lived, listening to Kent share his cosmic perspective on life day after day, I thought about a poem I had recently discovered called "Lapis Lazuli." W. B. Yeats's poem describes a semiprecious stone into which a picture has been carved. The picture shows two old Chinese men climbing a mountain path to a shrine where they will sit peacefully and look over the world spread out below. I thought about those two Chinamen a lot. I wanted to end my days like that, sitting in peaceful contemplation of the world, not reading newspapers with a magnifying glass while waiting for the canary to sing, like Other Mother, or smoking cigarettes, waiting for the ballgame to begin, like Bee Pa. One day in class I found myself, for the first time, unable to concentrate on what Kent was saying. Tumblers in my mind were falling into place, opening the door to what I hoped would be my future. Sitting in the gold circle of S-01, I decided what it was that I wanted out of life. I wanted to be like those two old Chinese men. I wanted to be wise. I wanted out of Plato's cave. I had only a vague notion of how I would find my way to the path that wound up that mountain. That vague notion gradually took the outlines of a hazy project that arose in my mind. I would learn about as many things as I could and thereby broaden my perspective as much as possible. Then I would choose one area of study and go deeper and deeper into it until … until what? Until I was deep? I could not foretell then how the project would end. I only knew that I would do whatever it took to be wise. Someday I would be like those two Chinamen, whose ancient glittering eyes were gay.

Plato set up his academy just outside Athens in an olive grove sacred to Athena, the goddess of wisdom. It lasted for eight hundred years. The last great philosopher to teach there was Proclus. Proclus's particular favorite among the gods was Athena, whom Plato called Theou Noesis—divine intelligence.

"Noesis" comes from the Greek "nous" and refers to knowledge that is apprehended directly, through intuition—the knowledge that is there when you need it, the truth that, once you hear it, sounds like something you have always known. Proclus believed that Athena guided him in moments of crisis. Imagine his excitement, then, when, upon hearing that the Christians had removed the statue of Athena from the Parthenon, Proclus had a dream in which he was told that Athena wanted to stay with him. The voice in the dream must have been speaking figuratively. Archaeologists have unearthed Proclus's home in Athens. There is no forty-foot statue of Athena in his living room. The gigantic statue was not removed to his home, however much Proclus may have wanted it. It may have been taken to Constantinople and was almost certainly destroyed. No one actually knows what became of it.

The history of the Parthenon itself is not so murky. Construction began in 447 BC and was completed nine years later. In the sixth century AD, the Parthenon became a Byzantine Christian church dedicated to Parthenos Maria, or Mary the Virgin. That Athena was also a virgin may or may not have entered the thinking of the church fathers when they named the church. The temple later became a Roman Catholic church, also dedicated to Mary. In 1458, the Ottoman Turks conquered Athens. They converted the Parthenon into a mosque and put a minaret inside it. They also put in a huge store of gunpowder. This pairing of the sacred and the profane worked about as well as it always has until September 28, 1687, when the Venetian army lobbed a mortar shell into the building. The remains of the minaret can still be seen. So can the remains of the Parthenon. In 1801, the British Earl of Elgin came to an alleged agreement with the Turks that allowed him to take whatever ruins he could fit into his boat. He sawed the larger chunks of the statuary groups into boat-sized pieces and made off with half the Parthenon marbles, later called the Elgin marbles after the British Museum bought them in 1816. The Greek government has been petitioning the government of England to return the statues since 1983, so far without success. Neither Greece nor England has asked for the plaster reproductions that line the perimeter of the Parthenon in Nashville.

Theou Noesis. Divine intelligence, intuitive consciousness, inner knowing. This was the result of Zeus's splitting headache. Athena was not born. She sprang full-grown from the forehead of Zeus, a single thought resplendent in armor, a fully formed idea that took shape in the quiet of the sky god's mind.

And the earth was without form, and void, and darkness was upon the face of the deep. In the beginning was the deep, the primordial abyss, the virgin womb, the blank slate, the quiet mind, from which any thought may arise once the spirit moves over the face of the waters.

From the depths of a pond, a lotus plant gropes toward the sunlight shining on the surface of the water. When it reaches the light, it blooms. From the depths of the mind, a thought forms and rises to the surface of consciousness, where it takes shape as a word. From the darkness upon the face of the deep, God says, and his words are the things themselves.

Kent sits at the edge of the circle in the floor of his classroom. He says that today we will dance our metaphors and asks who wants to go first. A student steps into the void. From the soles of his feet, his body sways up to his outstretched fingertips, undulating from ankles to crown, forward and backward, like a water plant in the eddy of a stream.

Pythia sits in the temple at Delphi, next to a chasm in the floor. Vapors from the chasm fill her nostrils as she peers into a bowl of sacred spring water. In the bowl, the answer to every question floats to the surface of the water.

Odin, king of the gods, hangs from the world tree, Yggsdrasil, a sacrifice of himself to himself, suspended over the well of wisdom, Mimisbrunnr, where long before he gave an eye in exchange for a single drink, an eye that stares back at him now from the depths of that well.

Galadriel pours water from a silver pitcher into the shallow basin of her magic mirror and asks Frodo to look inside.

Frodo peers into the basin and sees, forming in its depths, a vision of what is to come.

A man gazes at the backlit screen of a computer. He is still. As words rise up into his quiet mind, he types them onto the blank screen. Memories, facts, fantasies, and rumors take form, are arranged into patterns, are kneaded into stories.

What is creation but the act of attention? God sees a formless void. His attention moves across it, the spirit moving upon the face of the waters. A thought rises from the void and becomes light. A thought rises from the void and becomes dry land. God has only to speak the single word of attention—Behold!—and where there was nothing, there is being. From the lotus pond of the darkest, deepest void, from the bottomless, limitless, formless pool of potential, of nothing-yet-becoming that is God's mind, a thought rises like a frond from the muck below, and when it reaches the surface of full consciousness, it blooms. Into light. Into dry land. Into life.

These are Kent's program notes for Theater of the Mind's performance at ETC:

> What can one share now as one previously shared
> God? We can share man. And man is bread, and bread

is as it is. It does not hide. It does not package itself to look pretty. It does not ask to be accepted. But when it is eaten, it gives strength. This is not true of cake. Cake invites. Cake decorates itself. Cake packages itself. But when cake is eaten, it gives little sustenance.

Unfortunately, *they* are cake. But Grotowski says if the actor could be bread, he could truly share man in the theater, and he then would share man with his own life, with his own experiences, with his organic presence, with his skin, with everything that is under his skin, and with all the scars that life has left.

Kent booked Theater of the Mind to run for two weeks at ETC. Despite the fact that all the performers were high school students, word soon got out that Theater of the Mind was the most adventurous performance of any kind on view at that time in Nashville. An article about Theater of the Mind appeared in the local newspaper. At the end of two weeks we were still selling tickets. Kent booked the theater for an additional week and would have booked for longer, had the space been available.

In the storefront below ETC was a hippie shop that specialized in items of a spiritual nature. Displayed in the window was a book whose cover photograph featured an Indian man with dark, soulful eyes. His name was Meher Baba. One of the Prickly Heat Sisters, a delicately beautiful girl named Laura

Goode, saw me looking at the book one night before our performance. Laura reached into her enormous cloth bag and unexpectedly pulled out her own dog-eared copy of the book. Meher Baba never spoke, she said. He had stopped speaking because, after his enlightenment, he found that words got in his way. He did not want to be limited by the meanings of the words that were available to him. If there was something that he needed to communicate, he spelled it out on a small alphabet board that he carried with him.

Kent was a Catholic in every sense of the word. On the one hand, he rose every morning at 3:30 to say his daily office, then drove to the local Catholic church where he served as a lay minister. On the other hand, he practiced every other religion there was. One morning I saw Kent standing just outside the door of S-01 with a stack of square paperback books. As each of his students entered the room, Kent gave the student a book. I looked at my book as I lay on the gold carpet. The purple cover was etched with a circular design that I would later learn is called a mandala. Around the edge of the circle, written over and over again, were the words *Remember Be Here Now*. That, it turned out, was the title of Ram Dass's manual for living. The first part of the book describes how, in his former life as Harvard professor Richard Alpert, Ram Dass collaborated in Timothy Leary's ongoing experiments on the effects of LSD on human consciousness. That section goes on to describe his eventual meeting in India with the man who would become his guru. All that was interesting enough, but it was the next section of *Remember Be Here Now* that really grabbed me. It was printed sideways on what looked like brown wrapping paper. Its pages were crammed with Ram Dass's psychedelic doodles that illustrated the words that were handwritten in ornate script around, beside, over and under his pictures. There were pictures of Hindu gods. There were pictures of Jesus. There were pictures of the Buddha. The words and pictures were Ram Dass's attempt to express what he learned at the feet of his guru. Just as had happened to me only a few years before, a religious comic book had somehow landed in my lap. But where the religious pamphlets I read while singing with Just Us terrified me, Ram Dass's cartoons alternately baffled and thrilled me. *Remember Be Here Now* was a multifaith book. It was the first book I had ever seen that said outright what I had begun to suspect when I thought about the imaginary Hindu boy who had lived in my head since childhood: there is no one true religion.

Thumbing through the book again late that night, I took stock of my situation. When I arrived at McGavock, I was a very religious boy. From there, I had gone halfway to becoming a Jesus freak. Now, looking at the pictures Ram Dass had drawn of the gods and saints of every religion, I allowed into consciousness a thought that had been pushing up through the weeds of my mind all day: if I was willing to admit the possibility—and by now, it was nearer to being a certainty—that there was no one true religion, was I even still a Christian at all? I still believed there was a God, but what his name was, I could not rightly say.

Try to be more like Jesus. Or Socrates. Or Confucius, Siddhartha, Meher Baba. Pick one. Try to be more like anyone, from anywhere, as long as he is wiser than you.

Beth and Barnetta won. I started calling myself Michael, like everyone else did, and discovered that I liked the name. Then I took scissors and made a few careful cuts in my hair so that when I raked it back, it billowed out around my head in a storm cloud of dark waves, like the hair of the Vitruvian Man.

McGavock High School covered fourteen acres. There was so much ground to cover that students were allowed seven minutes between classes instead of the regulation five. Even so, I could not get to my locker more than once after my first stop in the morning. This meant hauling a mountain of books from class to class for what seemed like miles. It wasn't strictly necessary to add *Remember Be Here Now* to the load, but I put it on top of the stack anyway to announce to the world that I was on the road to enlightenment. So did Beth, whose class schedule was identical to mine. *Remember Be Here Now* replaced *The Teachings of Don Juan: A Yaqui Way*

of Knowledge on the top of my stack and was itself replaced in turn that year by *Zen and the Art of Archery, Jonathan Livingston Seagull,* and *Siddhartha*, among other books whose names I no longer recall.

One day a student teacher named Wes wandered over to the table that Beth and I shared in the back row of psychology class. Wes was a soft-spoken Vanderbilt student with a mustache and the longish hair that all the male student teachers had. Wes noticed the books we had carefully positioned on the top of our stacks. He stopped to ask about our interest in spiritual things and before long had pulled up a chair. It turned out that Wes had a guru. Wes's somber face lit up when he told us about Maharaj Ji, who was just then becoming famous—or infamous, depending on whom you asked. Every day thereafter, Wes would spend the last half of psychology class distracting Beth and me from our class exercises with his talk of the spiritual books he had read and the mystical states he had experienced. It quickly became clear to me that Wes was farther along the spiritual path than anyone I had yet known, so far down the path, in fact, that he appeared on the spiritual horizon as a lonely speck.

The big subject of debate in Theater of the Mind by that time was whether we had a guru of our own. I had many discussions about it with Barnetta in her car or mine as we drove home from school, and with Beth while skipping gym class after we figured out that showing up had no effect on our grade point averages. None of us quite knew what a guru was, but it seemed to many of us that Kent might be one. If a guru was a great teacher, then Kent was a guru. If a guru was someone who pointed out the meaning of life, then Kent was a guru. If a guru was someone who reverenced the sacred in all its forms, then Kent was a guru. Kent certainly looked like a guru in his turtleneck shirts and his suede vest with long suede fringe. Kent insisted that he was not a guru, but the fact that he had to repeat it spoke volumes about the position his students put him in.

One day Kent turned to me in class and pointed out that I had not volunteered to be in a format in several weeks. It was true. He asked if I was okay. I lied and said that I was.

The truth was that in the winter of 1973–74, the improvisations performed in S-01 were going through a period when they were more fact than fiction. The kids were becoming more and more comfortable revealing things about themselves that most never would have told their best friend before but now were sharing with a whole room full of people. I was not about to step into that public confessional. Instead, I waited it out, figuring it would not be long before these imaginative kids would be drawn back into the world of fiction, where I felt more comfortable. The problem was that I had something to hide. I was afraid that if I stepped into an arena where every soul was being bared, I would suddenly blurt out that I was gay.

Everybody knows the truism that the heirs of Jubal are pulled irresistibly to the theater. It had always been tacitly understood that there were real queers among the drama queers in Theater of the Mind and sometimes that tacit understanding would erupt into a ribald joke, as when Gerald in a scenario one day claimed to have kissed the Pope's ring, and Steven Welch counterclaimed to have kissed the Pope. I am sure that if any of the kids in Theater of the Mind are reading this book today, it comes as no surprise to them that I am gay. Which is just how I wanted it. I wanted to be truthful with my peers, but I felt more comfortable being truthful at a distance of thirty-five years. In the meantime, I watched fascinated as my classmates bared their souls and waited until they simply had nothing left to share. When I started doing improvs again, I steered every improv I was in toward comedy and away from any subject that might become remotely confessional. It became generally understood that I was not much good at being deep onstage. That was okay with me, since by that time the word "deep" had been so overworked that it had turned into Theater of the Mind's favorite joke. Nothing made us howl so loudly as the sight of Steven Welch sweeping downstage to puke the word "*deeeeep!*" into the laps of the front-row audience. Fiction became respectable once again in Theater of the Mind, and I kept my secrets to myself.

I dated girls like everybody else, but I wasn't even close to losing my virginity. I hadn't gotten past first base, hadn't even led off the bag. In those rare moments when I looked honestly into my heart, I could see that I wasn't in the game at all. One thing I did figure out: God made the Hindu boy just as he was and did not judge him for being Hindu. He would not judge me either for being gay. By the middle of my senior year in high school, I was quite certain that it was not God who objected to my true sexual orientation. I might object, but God did not. I was also sure that none of my friends in S-01 would object to it either. They might tease me if my secret got out, but they would not reject me. The only difficulties would be presented by my parents, my whole family, Hillhurst Baptist Church, all the neighbors, everybody else I had ever known, and the 2,976 other students at McGavock High School, some of whom might not let me out of the building alive. "God Knows I'm Good," sang David Bowie, and God knew that I was good. God did not care what my religion was, and he did not care that I was gay. But not everybody was as broadminded as God.

Once saved, always saved. It is a lucky thing, too. After walking the Christian straight-and-narrow all my life, I decided in my senior year to find out what kind of fun was available outside the bounds of respectability. At church, that amounted to nothing more than sitting in the back pew with kids who were more interested in each other than in what was happening at the altar. At school, I jumped neck deep into the kind of adventures that a teenager calls calculated risks and that his parents call shenanigans, if they ever find out about them.

I do not recall how the excuse pad fell into my possession. All I know now is that somehow or other, I had an official pad of get-out-of-class-free excuse slips. I had also inherited just enough artistic talent from my father to forge the signatures of several teachers. Every day before fourth period, I would set up shop like a medieval scribe in the carpeted circle of S-01, taking requests and writing out excuse slips for the performers of Theater of the Mind who wanted to skip a class. That went on for months, until I overreached by writing out two dozen slips at once for a field trip that Barnetta organized to a downtown restaurant.

Teasing, curious, skeptical Barnetta had become by that time the female star of S-01. That is not the same thing as saying that she was the class diva. That immense territory was occupied by a black singer/actress who would one day be named Zoe Walker. Barnetta, rather, was the provocateur who challenged Kent's theories and then was the first to test them out. Kent adored her and relied on her, as in some way we all did. To the extent that Theater of the Mind had a mother figure, it was Barnetta. She looked the part. Barnetta was tall like Beth, but unlike our slender friend, Barnetta was soft and full-figured. That is not to say that she was the earth-mother type that was so much esteemed in the hippie culture of those days. Barnetta was more a mother to us in the way that Wendy was a mother to the Lost Boys—the sort of girl who can say, "Now everybody into the water!" and everybody jumps. Which is what everybody did when she proposed a trip to the Gerst Haus.

The Gerst Haus was a German restaurant located on Woodland Street just across the river from downtown Nashville. Barnetta's second-favorite teacher, a redheaded lioness in a motorized wheelchair named Dr. Miriam Moore, mentioned it one day to her German class. When she heard about it, Barnetta became obsessed. She just had to have that German food. All we had to do, she said, was skip third, fourth and fifth periods, and we could go downtown to the Gerst Haus for lunch. We picked a day when Kent would be absent so as not to miss any doings in S-01. Barnetta drove that day. I sat in the passenger seat of her car, writing out excuse slips. Behind us stretched a parade of cars full of drama queers as well as the most part of the Prickly Heat Sisters. We found out the next day that the math geniuses had performed the Concerto for Briefcase and Book before third period as they always did, but to no audience whatsoever. All the other students in Dr. Currey's class were on their way to the Gerst Haus. Dr. Currey was livid. He knew perfectly well that we were up to something when two-thirds of his class failed to appear, but there was nothing he could do about it. Armed with the excuse slips I had written, all the young diners returned to school and slipped back into their routines without comment or incident. All, that is, except Beth and me. The teacher whose name I chose to sign on our behalf was out sick that day.

The next morning Beth and I were summoned to the principal's office, where Mack Hargis asked if we could think of one good reason why he should not suspend us from school that instant. Beth could think of several. She leveled her cool blue gaze on Mack Hargis. Not for nothing had she read *Gone with the Wind* twice.

"You can't suspend us," she informed Mack Hargis. "We're the people who keep McGavock's name in the newspapers." She then listed all the academic, dramatic and forensic titles we had won between us, some of which had indeed garnered favorable press for the school.

"Where are you going to college, young lady?" Principal Hargis asked.

"University of Tennessee," Beth said.

"What about you, son?"

"Princeton," I lied.

He looked at me carefully, but I did not gulp or flinch. He thought for a moment, long enough to realize we had him over a barrel. "Well, I'm going to let you off this time," he said by way of concluding the interview. "Just make sure you don't do it again." We assured him as we left his office that wild horses could not drag us away from our classes again.

There was one thing that morning that Principal Hargis forgot to do. Tucked inside the notebook that I carried when I left his office was the excuse pad, still in my possession. There were two blank slips left on it.

My cousin David was the first person in my family to go to college. He joined the navy when I was still a kid and then went to college on the GI Bill. I would be the second person in our family to go. For the champion of the honor roll, this was the moment of truth. Ever since I could remember, my mother had insisted that I study hard so that I could go to college. Ever since I could remember, my father had insisted that I study hard so that I could get a scholarship because there would not be enough money to pay for college. I had no doubt that I would get into a college someplace. The question was, would I be able to afford it?

I did well on the SATs. Not astronomical numbers by any means but respectable for Tennessee, whose public education system at that time was ranked fiftieth in the nation. Over the summer I had begun to receive brochures from colleges all over the country soliciting my application. The first brochure to arrive came from West Point. At that time I did not know there would be other brochures to follow, so for a week I imagined myself as the sort of boy who would flourish at a military academy. The next brochure came from St. John's, and for another week I fantasized about how wise I would become if I read all the Great Books. Soon the trickle of brochures turned into a torrent. Every day the mailbox at 2900 Rich Acres Drive was stuffed with more brochures. After a while I barely glanced at them. By autumn I had already made up my mind to keep it simple and apply to the University of Tennessee at Knoxville, which with scholarships and low in-state tuition, I would be able to afford.

One brochure was for a college so strange that I did not throw it away immediately but showed it to my friends in S-01 the next day. They thought it was hilarious, as did I. We laughed and laughed when we tried to imagine who would be dumb enough to go to an all-male school with only twenty-six students in the middle of the desert, where drugs and alcohol were strictly forbidden and the nearest town where you could buy any was twenty-five miles away and reached only by driving over a mountain pass. When class started, we did a scenario that we titled *The Voice of the Desert*, which was what the founder of Deep Springs College said you could hear if you listened closely enough to the vast nothingness of Deep Springs Valley.

Lucien Lucius ("L. L.") Nunn established Deep Springs College in 1917 using the fortune he made bringing electricity to the mines of the American West. Nunn's interest in education was purely practical at first. Unable to lure engineers from the East to work under the frontier conditions out west, Nunn recruited tough young locals for the job and educated them himself. He devised an educational system that went far beyond what his workers needed to keep his electrical plants running. Nunn's system placed equal weight on three things: academics, physical labor, and self-governance of the student body. Gradually, Nunn became more interested in his unique educational system and the future leaders of the nation he believed it would produce than in the running of his utilities. A stockholder revolt forced Nunn out of his company and shut down his educational experiment. Liberated from his managerial duties, with a pile of money in the bank and a passion for education in his heart, Nunn cast about for a place where he could set up an even more daring demonstration of his educational ideals. His search led him to the Swinging

T, a ranch located in a remote California valley called Deep Springs.

"Remote" only begins to describe Deep Springs Valley. The valley is a mile-high bowl of desert between the Inyo and White Mountains. It measures approximately twenty-three square miles, about the size of Manhattan. The college Nunn founded at the Swinging T is separated from the nearest town by twenty-five miles of mountain road and is forty miles away from the nearest town of consequence, Bishop, California. There are only two things in Deep Springs Valley. Deep Springs College is one of them. The other is Deep Springs Lake, a shallow body of salt water at the southern end of the valley that dries to a salt pan in summer. The rest is sage, cactus, and tumbleweed.

It was Deep Springs' isolation that Theater of the Mind found so hilarious that day. L. L. Nunn had taken advantage of the remote setting of his new school to add two new ground rules to his educational experiment. The first was the isolation policy. No student was allowed to leave the valley during term unless for school or ranch business, emergencies or religious services. The second ground rule was the real knee-slapper: no drugs or alcohol permitted to students in the valley—period, ever. My friends rolled on the carpet and howled when I read that out loud. For all I knew, some of them were high when they heard it. After all, fourth period did not begin until 10:00 in the morning. Surely someone had fired up a doobie by then.

I had been a total Christian square right up through the

end of junior year. Even in Kentucky the summer after, when I was part of a summer stock company that was notorious for its debauchery, I got up and went to church every Sunday morning but the last. Back in Nashville that fall, I decided that it was time to join in all the fun my friends in S-01 were having. After I tried beer, wine, vodka, rum, Southern Comfort, marijuana, hashish, Quaaludes, Valium, Darvon, PCP, MDA, THC, LSD, and mescaline, I wondered what it was that I had been so afraid of. This stuff was great!

By the time I started applying to college, I had been to some great parties. At only one was I sober, an impromptu gathering at Hammelbacher following a performance of *Antigone,* when Doug fetched his marimba down from the attic to play Bach for us. Kent, Ruth and Doug collaborated on a production of *Antigone* at a community theater called the Circle. Kent directed, Doug designed sets, and Ruth starred in the title role. Barnetta, Beth, Steven Welch, Ricky Santry and I were cast in the chorus and Gerald was cast as Tiresias the blind seer, which meant that we were invited to all the swell parties that the adult cast members attended. There was a party at the apartment of a Vanderbilt professor who served port and sherry, which tasted great once you smoked some pot. There was a costume party for which the host, an impossibly handsome Adonis who made the costumes for the show, refused to give us the address. "It's on Belmont Boulevard," he said. "You'll find it." As Barnetta inched her car down the boulevard, we passed a large bungalow where, under a spotlight on the porch, was positioned a dressmaker's dummy with gladiolas stuffed into the arm and neck holes. The Adonis met us at the door on roller skates and with a joint in his mouth from which he shotgunned each of us before skating off to tend to his other guests. There were parties at kids' houses when their parents were out of town. There were all-night acid parties in the bushes of the state park. There were parties in the homes of people we had never met, and parties in the lighting booth of McGavock Theater in the middle of the day, and lunch parties on the lawn of the historic mansion next door to the school. When there were no parties to go to, we took mescaline and went to Kmart. When we had no drugs, we used our fake IDs and went to bars downtown, where we taught ourselves to drink scotch like grown-ups instead of ordering the daiquiris we really wanted. As far as I knew, all this was a normal part of growing up, since by that time everyone I knew was having pretty much the same or a similar experience—I had been the last holdout for stone-cold sobriety. If every teenager in America was taking drugs and drinking like I was, where was Deep Springs College going to find thirteen entering freshmen who would put up with its ground rules?

A week later I was not laughing. Something else in that brochure had caught my eye. It was the word "free." L. L. Nunn had stipulated when he established it that Deep Springs College would not charge its students for their education. An education at Deep Springs was free. No tuition, no charge for room and board, nothing. All a student had to pay for were travel, books and incidentals. Deep Springs was too small to offer a four-year degree, but if I started school there, my first two years of college would cost nothing.

I would have been ashamed to have such a venal motive for applying if there had not been something else at work in my mind as well. The words of L. L. Nunn printed in the brochure were slowly working their alchemy on me. "Great leaders in all ages have sought the desert and heard its voice." All my life I had worshipped a Savior who lived in a desert or something like one. Every image of holiness I had ever seen was an image set on sand. Truth to tell, I was ready to trade a life of parties for something more essential. I still went to church every Sunday, but the ties that bound me to my Christian faith were coming loose. If I were ever to find something to take their place, Deep Springs seemed like as good a place as any to start looking. I filled out the application form and got to work on the ten essay questions it asked. I no longer knew quite what to make of Jesus, but when I received my acceptance letter from Deep Springs, I decided to follow him into the wilderness. My father called the school to make sure there were no Communists there. Once he was satisfied, I began planning my trip to Deep Springs. I looked forward to becoming a hermit. I would go to Deep Springs and live the life of the mind. I would listen to the voice of the desert and learn whatever it had to teach me.

One day near the end of the school year, Wes came to the back row of psychology class with a stack of books in his arms. He gave half of them to Beth and half to me. His face was luminous when he told us that he had decided to leave Vanderbilt, a month shy of getting his degree, to follow Maharaj Ji. He had only a few possessions left to give away and then he would leave, probably the next day. We never saw Wes again.

I still have one of Wes's books. It is called *The Zen Teachings of Huang Po*. Here is the first paragraph of the book:

> The Master said to me: All the Buddhas and all sentient beings are nothing but the One Mind, beside which nothing exists. This Mind, which is without beginning, is unborn and indestructible. It is not green nor yellow, and has neither form nor appearance. It does not belong to the categories of things which exist or do not exist, nor can it be thought of in terms of new or old. It is neither long nor short, big nor small, for it transcends all limits, measures, names, traces and comparisons. It is that which you see before you—begin to reason about it and you at once fall into error. It is like the boundless void which cannot be fathomed or measured. The One Mind alone is the Buddha, and there is no distinction between the Buddha and sentient things, but that sentient beings are attached to forms and so seek externally for Buddhahood. By their very seeking they lose it, for that is using the Buddha to seek for the Buddha and using mind to grasp Mind. Even though they do their utmost for a full aeon, they will not be able to attain to it. They do not know that, if they put a stop to conceptual thought and forget their anxiety,

the Buddha will appear before them, for this Mind is Buddha and the Buddha is all living beings. It is not the less for being manifested in ordinary beings, nor is it greater for being manifested in the Buddhas.

I could not make heads or tails of it. I closed the book after reading that paragraph and put it among my other books, where it remained, untouched and yellowing, for thirty-three years.

By the time David Bowie announced his Diamond Dogs tour, he was a much bigger star than he had been when I saw him at the War Memorial Auditorium. This time around he would bring his show into the much larger Municipal Auditorium, where I worked as an usher. I was ecstatic—until I took a closer look at the date: Saturday, June 29. I was supposed to be at Deep Springs on Saturday, June 29. Deep Springs had the peculiar practice of starting in early summer because students were needed to buck the bales of hay that were harvested in summer from the alfalfa fields. The Saturday before classes began was devoted to a tour of Deep Springs Valley, the ranch, and the college. I would be in California riding around in the back of a cattle truck while the drama queers were dressing for the concert.

To make matters worse, my friends Jason and Steve announced that they were going to meet Bowie when he came to town. They had no actual invitation to do so, nor any kind of plan, but I knew better than to dismiss their claims out of

THE THOUSAND-PETALED LOTUS

hand. Steve had a beautiful, resonant voice that had landed him a part-time gig reading news for a local radio station. He had another job as well, working as a table magician at an expensive restaurant. Steve was only seventeen, but he was already the best magician in Nashville. He figured there would be a way to parlay one or another of his part-time jobs into an opportunity to meet Bowie. Jason had no ready-made platform to build on like Steve did, but he was easily creative enough to devise a hundred ways of meeting Bowie by June. It was Jason who had figured out how to smoke pot from a bong while driving. It was Jason who had a dream one night that revealed to him the perfect method of shoplifting albums from record stores; by his junior year his record collection was fabled. It was Jason who had rigged up the flash pots for my terrifying entrance as Mephistopheles in our production of *Dr. Faustus.* Jason was a superb mime, and if he could sneak on to the stage, no one would ever know that he was not part of the show.

I could not bear the thought that Steve and Jason would meet Bowie while I would not. Jason and Steve were straight, and while they were androgynous to the extent that every interesting young man was androgynous in those days, they simply did not understand what it was to love Bowie as I did. There was no way I would listen to them tell their stories of meeting Bowie without having one of my own. Thus began the three-way contest to meet David Bowie.

The hope that I might win that contest brought up what I imagined at the time to be a legitimate question: what if the famous bisexual wanted to have sex with me? My hair looked great and I had started doing pushups, so it seemed reasonable to think that an internationally famous rock-and-roll star might want to have sex with a legal-aged teenager whose freckles were finally fading and who was considered by his classmates to be more attractive than not. I gazed at the picture of David Bowie and Twiggy on the cover of his latest album, *Pin Ups*. I imagined a sleek hotel room with crisp white sheets spread over an enormous bed. Then I added one tiny detail to the sexual identity I had invented for myself earlier that year. I would be bisexual. I would be celibate. But if David Bowie asked me to have sex with him, I would say yes.

Two weeks before the end of the school year, Beth and I wandered into S-01 during Kent's free period, clutching my last two excuse slips. We had just returned from a drive out to the Cumberland River for what we had decided to call a coffee break. Kent took one look at our red-rimmed glassy eyes and said, "Oh, my fallen angels, the whole school is looking for you! They're announcing the senior award winners. You must go to the cafeteria immediately. They're waiting on you!" These were not ideal circumstances in which to be stoned. When we got to the cafeteria, I reminded myself that I had read *Gone with the Wind*, arched an eyebrow, pushed open the door and imagined that I was Scarlett, forced by Rhett to wear a red velvet ball gown to confront Melanie Hamilton when the whole world knew I had just tried to seduce her husband. But instead of a smiling Melanie wafting toward me with outstretched arms saying, "Look, here's our Scarlett," what I saw were fifty students arrayed in front of a podium where Dr. James Curry was leaning into a microphone. "Ah, we can begin at last," his voice boomed. "Michael and Beth have just arrived, courtesy of the Gerst Haus." The fact that everyone laughed was evidence of just how far news of the previous month's adventure had traveled. We laughed right along with them. So did Dr. Curry. We learned that day that the senior honors awards for English would be bestowed by Dr. Currey on Beth and me. Barnetta, Gerald, Chris Wilson, and the future Zoe Walker would receive English department awards for theater. Dr. Currey harbored no ill will toward us, and we had none for him. We would not break any more rules. The excuse pad was used up anyway. That was okay. The school year was almost over. No more excuses would be needed.

Theater of the Mind gave its last performance at a festival on the lawn of the Parthenon. It was June. Everyone who was going to college knew where they would be in September and everyone else was just grateful to be getting out of high school. We could not have performed one more time. The weather was warm, we were graduating, the magnolias were in bloom. We were too giddy with excitement to focus on anything for more than five minutes. This was the last time that Kent would ever be able to round us up and calm us down long enough to perform. All our youthful excitement, all our hopes and dreams, went into that performance. The climax of the show came when Steven

Welch knelt in front of Beth with his back to her, stuck his head up into her red peasant blouse, and pressed his face against the fabric so that she looked pregnant with a full-grown human head. For the next three minutes, the bizarre fetus prophesied from Beth's swollen belly. The show ended when Beth gave Steven a push and he landed in a ball on the lawn, bawling like a newborn. Our good-byes after that were lingering and tinged with sadness. We would see each other the following week at school and at graduation, but we would be Theater of the Mind no longer. Slowly we split up into pairs and small groups to leave. I asked Barnetta to wait for me just a minute and then climbed the steps to the Parthenon where, for the last time, I dropped all the money I had into the slot beneath the tiny bronze statue of the goddess of wisdom.

Proclus believed that he was guided by Athena. We do not know what guidance the goddess of wisdom gave him. Was it what we call the still, small voice within? Was it what Baptists call the Holy Spirit? Did Athena give advice? Direction? Or did she offer only a gentle reminder to begin each moment at the beginning?

Meister Eckhardt said one must leave God to find God. What did Jesus leave when he went into the wilderness? What did he find there? What did he bring back?

Before there was Christianity, there was the Way. That is what Jesus's early followers called his teachings in the years immediately after his Crucifixion. Christianity had not yet been invented. There was no religion built up around a Savior in those first few years. There was only a shining example, a body of teachings, and feelings of loss, excitement and wonder. There were no Christians then. There were only followers of the Way. Jesus of Nazareth had walked among them and shown them the Way.

What Way did Jesus teach? What road leads back to God? Where can one find the directions to the path that climbs the mountain where God is found? Does the Holy Ghost whisper them in your ear? Did Athena? Or does any track, traveled far enough, become the Way to the Chinamen's shrine?

Our final main-stage production at McGavock was *The Tragicall History of the Life and Death of Doctor Faustus* by Christopher Marlowe. I played Mephistopheles in a Renaissance doublet and a white fright wig. Every night for five weeks of rehearsal and one week of performance, I recited the words that more and more echoed my own thoughts about where I had begun in life and where I was now:

Why this is hell, nor am I out of it.
Think'st thou that I who saw the face of God,
And tasted the eternal joys of heaven,
Am not tormented with ten thousand hells,
In being depriv'd of everlasting bliss?

I had endured the loss of my deeply religious life. I had further admitted to myself that I might no longer be a follower of Christ at all. The only thing left to me of my old religion was God himself. Now I was starting to wonder if he would be the next thing I would have to do without.

The first thing I did was to call the head usher at the Municipal Auditorium to tell him that I was available to work the night of the Bowie concert. I had not worked in a while because my schedule was so full of play rehearsals and performances, but the head usher was happy to hear from me and said that he could use me that night. Jason, Steve and I had made plans to sit together, so I already had a ticket for a premium seat ten rows from the stage. The last thing I had to do before planning my outfit was to call the dean at Deep Springs to tell him that I would be unavoidably delayed in my arrival and could not possibly get there before Sunday afternoon. He was very understanding.

As always on the night of a concert, I got to my station in the mezzanine well before any spectators arrived. I was in luck. As happened only occasionally, the band was onstage setting up before the show. I had gambled that Bowie would be in the auditorium before the show and not locked away in his dressing room or zonked out at his hotel or riding from the airport in a limousine or being in any of a dozen other places where a rock star might be just before a show. There he was, on stage, calling down to the lighting designer, consulting with the stage hands, doing all the things a director does before a show, just as I had seen Kent do a hundred times. My plan was going to work. I was terrified.

I left my station and went down to the front of the stage. Bowie seemed to be winding up his preparations and was crossing the stage, heading for the wings. I swallowed hard and said, "Mr. Bowie, would you have a moment to meet one of your biggest fans?" He turned and smiled, came to the edge of the stage, shook my hand and sat down. "Nice place you've got here," he said.

I was awestruck. Unfortunately, I was also dumbstruck. Here he was, sitting right in front of me, ready to have a real conversation with one of his fans, and I couldn't think of a single thing to say. I asked him for his autograph and he gave it to me. Finally I mustered up the courage to speak the truth. I said to him, very quietly, "Wow, what do you say to a real live rock-and-roll star?" He smiled and nodded his head. He was very kind. It probably was not the first time something like this had happened to him. He stood up, shook my hand and told me it was nice to meet me, then trotted backstage to get dressed.

I had to get dressed, too. I abandoned my station, went back to the room where the maroon blazers of the ushers were kept, took off my blazer and hung it up. Then I went out to the parking lot where my car was waiting. I wriggled around in the backseat until I had donned the outfit I had stashed there. The usher who took my ticket when I reentered the auditorium smiled and laughed when he saw me. I walked into the auditorium wearing an embroidered shirt, my trusty platform shoes, a floor-length purple cape and a top hat. My friends were already there by then, with no stories to tell about meeting Bowie. I told them mine and then we enjoyed the concert together. I felt no pressure in my chest, no longing to be near him even though Bowie had never looked handsomer than he did that night in his white suit and blue sweater. Halfway through the concert, I got up to leave. The only flight I had been able to book that would get me to California before classes started on Monday was a redeye that left Saturday night. I hugged my friends good-bye and set off through the crowd, my purple cape flowing out behind me. I was happy that I had met Bowie, relieved that he did not ask me to run away with him, and excited at the prospect of the adventure ahead of me. That drive to the airport was the start of life on my own, away from my family, away from Nashville, away from Hillhurst Baptist Church. I had stayed at the concert as long as I could and barely made it to the airport on time. I was the last person to get on the plane. I was so late that my seat had already been given to someone on standby. The flight attendant just smiled and bumped me up to first class, the only time that has ever happened to me. I was the only person in the first class cabin that night. I ordered a scotch and settled in for my very first flight on an airplane.

I showed up at Deep Springs College on Sunday evening in the middle of dinner, wearing a top hat and platform shoes. When I walked into the boardinghouse, the other students looked up from their meals to take in the new arrival and I knew immediately that I had woefully miscalculated my wardrobe. Even the new students were grungy, unshaven and uncombed, and they had only been there a day and a half. I had made sure to have a change of clothes for the Bowie concert when I started this adventure the day before but had neglected to set out a ripped T-shirt and some rotten sneakers to change into on the Greyhound bus that brought me up the Owens Valley from Los Angeles. I did have the wit to stuff my purple cape into my suitcase before I checked it at the airport, but the top hat would not fit. Sunday dinner at Deep Springs was always served buffet style from all the leftovers of the previous week. The student who had driven me over Westgard Pass kindly pointed out which dishes had been good and which were best left alone, then quickly heaped his plate with the good stuff and took a seat. I was left alone at the buffet table where I served myself, the only person standing in the room and the tallest, since I needed both hands to fill my plate and therefore could not take off my hat. I took an empty seat at one of the tables of six and introduced myself. There was no place to put my hat. I decided just to wear it for the remainder of the meal in the hope that the other students would start to feel ridiculous without one.

After dinner, my roommate, an easygoing fellow named Ken Kaufman who had a cloud of long dark hair like mine, introduced himself and showed me our room before trotting off to play volleyball with his twin brother, Bill, and most of the other students. I put on my oldest T-shirt and joined some other students in the main room, where I picked over the magazines—*Scientific American*, *Partisan Review*, *Paris Review*, *Co-Evolution Quarterly*, and other highbrow periodicals that I had barely heard of. I knew that Deep Springs attracted intellectual heavyweights from high schools all over America and beyond, so I was not surprised by the reading material on offer, just daunted by all the intellectual catching up that I would have to do. I said good night early and went back to my room.

After unpacking, I sat down to write a letter to my family announcing my safe arrival. Out of the corner of my eye I saw what I thought was a piece of brown grocery sack on the arm of the chair next to me. I absentmindedly reached over to brush it off, and it moved. I looked at it again. It was a scorpion. I yelped and ran into the room across the hall, where earlier I had seen the president of the student body, a scrappy bespectacled pixie named J. Michael Perez, reading a book. J. Michael calmly walked into my room, dropped an open jar over the scorpion, slid a book cover under it, walked out of the building, and released the monster into the desert.

Lying in bed that night, looking out the window at the moonlit desert, I took stock of my situation. I had not been at Deep Springs even six hours and already my reputation was in flames. I had to do something, and fast.

The first time anybody at Deep Springs asked me about my religious beliefs, I threw God under the bus and declared that I was an agnostic. It was true, anyway. With three thousand miles between me and my family, me and Hillhurst Baptist Church, me and the Buckle of the Bible Belt, the slender cord that bound me to my faith had snapped. I was not cocky enough to say that I was an atheist; I did not think I had enough evidence one way or the other to say that God did or did not exist. Uncertainty about the existence of God seemed like a more honest stance to me. I had done much thinking about God over the last year. Every religion had an equal claim on God, and like the five blind men feeling the elephant, each described God in its own way. From a religious perspective, there was an objective thing called God, who was described and worshipped differently in different cultures. But suppose the elephant was not an elephant at all but only a statue of an elephant? The five blind men would still describe an elephant. From a humanist perspective, all those different religions were attempts to explain creation and to meet the basic human need for order in the universe. Did not science do the same for us in the modern era, without reference to a supreme being pulling levers behind the scene? It seemed just as possible to me that man had created God as that God had created man. I could not choose between the two perspectives, so I hedged my bets. I became an agnostic.

Being an agnostic put me on a respectable intellectual footing with the other students. It meant that I was on my way to living the life of the mind, which was the goal of every Deep Springs student at the time. The life of the mind and how to live it was the subject of countless heated discussions carried out while drinking coffee in the morning before classes or working around the ranch in the afternoon or drinking herbal tea in the boardinghouse at night. We esteemed it as a lifelong intellectual adventure that required the courage to abandon any theory, any belief, that could not stand the test of reason. The life of the mind required of a young intellectual the same total commitment that a Poor Theater required of an actor or that salvation required of a Christian.

Deep Springers would make a second cup of tea, and a jar of peanut butter would be fetched from the pantry when the debate shifted, around eleven at night, to which great thinker was the best role model for the life of the mind. The frontrunner seemed to be Friedrich Nietzsche, but that may have been because his champion in the student body drank more tea and stayed up later than anyone else. If anybody asked me what I thought, I would hem and haw a bit and then say, "Plato," but only because nobody else at Deep Springs had ever heard of Jerzy Grotowski. I did not care too much one way or the other who the role model was, as long as there was someone I could try to be like other than myself. That was nothing new to me. I had started out life trying to be like Jesus. In Theater of the Mind, I wanted to be like Ryszard Cieslak. At Deep Springs, I exchanged Cieslak, the actor and artist who performed the plays, for Grotowski, the intellectual and artist who directed them, ran the theater, and wrote the books. I decided that when I grew up, I would start a theater company in America like Grotowski's Polish Laboratory Theater, one in which theater would be pared down to its essence and whose aim would be a kind of holiness.

The truth was that by the winter of my first year at Deep Springs, I was secretly longing to have something sacred in my life once again. I enjoyed the gloss of intellectual respectability that agnosticism lent me at Deep Springs. I did not enjoy doubt. The gnawing uncertainty of agnosticism was not nearly as warm a companion in the middle of the night as Christian faith. I still went with my family to church on breaks from school, but I could no more stuff myself back into the mold of Christian faith than I could have wriggled my growing muscles into the embroidered shirts and drive-in-movie pants that were still hanging in my closet back in Nashville. I could not go backward, and I was not comfortable where I was. For two years I said nothing to my friends at Deep Springs about my desire for some sort of truth that would not shift beneath my feet. Then, in May of 1976, just before I left Deep Springs, I had an experience that ended my agnosticism once and for all.

Over Christmas break, the garage where our vehicles were maintained was destroyed by fire. The cinder block shell of the walls remained, but the roof was gone and everything inside was ruined. My last labor assignment at the college was to assist in the rebuilding of the garage. I helped frame out the two rooms and rewire the building. Ken and I shingled the new roof. I was not thinking about God or the lack thereof very much. I was happy at Deep Springs. I had not heard the voice of the desert and was no closer to knowing what Jesus found when he went into the wilderness than I was when I arrived, but even so, the desert was beautiful. I loved the way that every plant had a clean space around it where I could see the sand. I loved the green oases of the alfalfa fields, the big cottonwood trees growing between the dirt roads and the irrigation ditches, the way that the front doors of the small stone faculty cottages opened onto the green lawn of the circular campus, while the back doors opened into the desert. The days were getting longer, allowing more time to linger in the flowering spring desert, more time to talk and laugh in the warm evening air, more time to lie on the grass circle and look at the stars, which were brighter there than at any place I have ever been, and more time to wish that there was more time. I had arrived at the ranch incongruously dressed in a top hat and platform shoes. Now I looked like the other students. My long hair was tied back with a leather thong. I wore straight-legged jeans, heavy work boots, and a bandanna around my head in the afternoons to keep the sweat out of my eyes. I had not listened to David Bowie in over a year. I had become fond of Joni Mitchell, and in May 1976, my favorite song was "California," a place that I was sad to be leaving.

One warm May afternoon, I was in the garage pushing a board across a table saw. Ken was working nearby. I had sawn the board halfway through when in a moment, somehow, everything became inexplicably, mysteriously right. The world took on an entirely new and fresh aspect to me. I saw and understood in that moment that the board and the saw, that the act of sawing and he who sawed, could no more be separated from something called God than what we call God could be separated from anything else. Somehow in that moment it became clear to me that sawing a board could not happen independently of God, that this thing called sawing, this garage, this person and this place, could not exist were there not something that held all this together and made it whole.

I said nothing to Ken about that flash of clarity even though he was working just a few feet away. I said nothing about it to anyone at dinner that night and nothing the next day. I saw no need to tell my classmates that my faith had returned in an experience that I could not explain, that I could barely find words for, that was both irrational and undeniable. The experience was not consistent with the life of the mind. My conviction that God was real would not stand the test of reason. I knew that God was real, but I had to admit to myself that I did not know the first thing about him ... or it. Faced with a choice, I said good-bye to the life of the mind. A week or so later, I said good-bye to Deep Springs as well. Another student drove me over Westgard Pass to Big Pine where I caught the

Greyhound Bus into Los Angeles. As the truck crossed the cattle guard at the edge of the campus, the dinner bell was rung, as it always is when a student leaves Deep Springs for the last time.

Three months later I set down my suitcase, took off my backpack, and looked around the quad at Columbia University, where I would finish my education, have sex with a man who wasn't David Bowie, and come out of the closet at last. Up to that time I had lived my youth in close-knit circles of likeminded young people who shared a common purpose. There were the prayer circles of Just Us, the sunken circle in the center of Room S-01 where Theater of the Mind began, and the small circle of stone buildings at Deep Springs that turned their backs on the desert and huddled around a fragile grass lawn. At Columbia, everything was rectangles and squares. I looked up at the neoclassical facade of Butler Library and saw the names carved into the frieze above the columns: Homer, Herodotus, Sophocles, Plato, Aristotle, Demosthenes, Cicero, Virgil. If there was a church of man, this was surely its high temple. Here, man would be the measure of all things. By that time, I had lost my desire to worship in any temple, whether of man, God, or anyone else. I had left God behind and followed Jesus into the wilderness, and there I found God. I found it everywhere.

In 1990, a full-scale replica of the ancient statue of Athena was unveiled in the Parthenon. Nashville's Athena is as historically accurate as possible. Sculptor Alan LeQuire's design is based on careful study of the surviving accounts of the original statue as well as on scholarship pertaining to statuary of the time. Like all Greek statues as they originally appeared, the statue of the goddess of wisdom is polychrome, or painted. Athena's armor and tunic are gilt. Her hair is blonde, her eyes are blue, her lips are pink, her cheeks are rouged and her eyelashes are three inches long and made of gold. She looks right at home in Music City, USA. Athena Parthenos is the largest indoor sculpture in the Western world. She is worth every penny that I gave for her as a child.

David Bowie was inducted into the Rock and Roll Hall of Fame in 1996. Around that time he made a movie called *Basquiat* in which he played Andy Warhol. My partner designed the costumes. John enjoyed working with Bowie. When I asked him why, what he told me was that David Bowie is a very kind man.

S-01 today is the strangest-looking classroom in America. The room has blackboards and desks, just like any other classroom, but the desks are crowded to one side of an open pit in the center of the room. There is a curved wall at one end of the room that hides the junk that has accumulated behind it over the years. In one corner of the room is a small lighting booth. Theatrical lights hang from the ceiling, waiting to illuminate a performance that is not in rehearsal and that no one will ever give.

Of the six actors in Theater of the Mind who later moved to New York City, only I remain.

Zoe Walker joined the cast of the hit Broadway show *Ain't Misbehavin'*. Finding little acting work for overscaled black women after that, she moved into arts administration and now lives in upstate New York.

Gerald Hyland fell in love with a coworker at the hotel switchboard where he worked. Rodney was one of the early victims of AIDS. Gerald cared for Rodney until he died, then returned to Nashville and became a nurse.

Despite his sincere best efforts, Steven Welch never succeeded in destroying himself. He shared a townhouse with a vice president of one of New York's major publishing houses, then retired with him to their cottage in Southampton. Steven's care enabled his partner to die in his own home. Steven lives there still, happily though with no visible means of support. He has helped countless lost souls find a foothold in sanity where once his own was so perilous.

Beth Brown did indeed attend the University of Tennessee at Knoxville but only for a year. She graduated from New York University and married a man who died young, leaving her with two beautiful children and a last name that suits her: DeVoe. Beth returned to Nashville to raise her children and still lives there today.

Barnetta Carter was my lifelong best enemy for the length of her life, not mine. After appearing in numerous Off-Off-Broadway, back alley and street theater productions in the city, she moved upstate and found her true calling, which was arts in education. Barnetta went from classroom to classroom in Rochester, helping teachers engage their students by creating theatrical experiences that brought the curriculum to life. The last time I saw her she was back in New York, serving for one year as interim director of the HB Studio for actors. When her stint at HB was up, she returned to Rochester. She missed teaching. She was also finding it difficult to work at all. Her memory was failing. Barnetta died March 4, 2010, from complications of diabetes.

Ruth Sweet completed her PhD in theater at Florida State University. She returned to Nashville, married a prominent lawyer, opened an acting school, and made a pile of money teaching communication skills to Nashville executives. The last time I saw her, she showed me a print of a Magritte painting that she had given to Kent. "What do you see when you look at that picture?" she asked. I described the picture, a painting of a landscape seen through a window. "Look at it again," she said. I looked at it again and saw that what I took to be a straightforward picture of a landscape seen through a window was actually a painting *of a painting* of a landscape seen through a window. "So that Kent will remember that the world is not what you think it is," she said. She did not say anything about lung cancer. Maybe she was unaware of it at the time. We talked about it on the telephone a few months later. Ruth died on August 25, 1998.

Doug Williams became a painter on a dare. One day Kent presented him with a magnificent book on modern art. Doug flipped quickly through the book and said, "Oh, I could do that." Kent's response was, "Why don't you?" Doug bought canvas, brushes, and oils, then spent the last decade of his life in a creative frenzy. A couple of his early paintings hang in my apartment today. They are as fearless as he was.

On his frequent visits to New York in the 1990s, Doug would call and ask me to go with him to church. I would meet him in the evening at his Midtown hotel and then we would take a taxi to the corner of Forty-Sixth Street and Broadway. There, behind a Howard Johnson's restaurant, was the door to the Gaiety Male Burlesque. We would climb the flight of stairs to the tiny box office, where we would pay the proprietress ten dollars apiece, then take a swing through the Apollo Lounge to see who was dancing that night, and finally take seats in the dim little theater, as close to the runway stage as we could get. As we waited for the first dancer to part the curtain of silver streamers at the back of the stage, Doug would descant on the significance of the lingam and the holiness of the ancient rite to the mighty god Priapus. "There is no symbol of life more potent," he would say as the house lights dimmed and the deejay cranked up the disco beat. "It's the oldest religion in the world." Doug died of a heart attack on July 7, 2001.

Kent Cathcart still lives in the apartment that was the scene of so many excited gatherings and so much of my education when I was young. He rises early every morning and recites his daily office, then meditates for the rest of the morning in a small room that he has devoted to that purpose. There are photographs of Ruth Sweet and Doug Williams on the walls of that room, as well as pictures of the deities and saints of every religion. Another room is now given over to his collection of Tibetan singing bowls, said to be the largest in North America. Ranged around the room are seventy or more bowls of various sizes, each on its own silk pillow. Ask him and Kent will play them for you. While you relax with your eyes closed, he will strike and stir the bowls with a mallet, summoning from each the pure primordial song that first filled the cosmic void. It is the sound from which the first word was formed, a sound that leads the mind back to the place of stillness before ideas take shape, before thoughts arise.

Framed on the shelf above my desk is the Christmas card my mother sent me last year. It is a picture of the Parthenon. Ranged on the lawn in front of it is a nativity scene that was set up each year during the 1960s by Harvey's Department Store. The nativity scene was enormous, almost a football field in length. Its life-size white plaster figures included not only the holy family seated under the star of Bethlehem but also the wise men and their camels, the shepherds and their animals, a host of angels and a grove of palm trees, all arranged before a white plaster forest of bare-limbed trees. The Harvey's nativity scene was my favorite thing about Christmas. Every December, after Kim, Miles, and I had submitted our final revised Christmas lists, my father would drive our family through downtown Nashville to Centennial Park. Leaving our car parked just inside the entrance, we would walk across the crunchy frost-covered grass toward the Parthenon, shining on its raised terrace, until we reached the nativity scene spread out below it. There, with our breath visible on the air in front of us, my family would watch in wonder as colored spotlights along the ground turned the pure-white figures blue; then red, green, and yellow; then white again, while behind them the temple of the goddess of wisdom glowed golden in the dark winter night. The Christmas card is a reminder of two virgin births—one of the wisdom that stepped fully formed from the silence of the sky god's mind, that void where an inkling grows into a thought before blossoming as a word; the other of the Word that was with God and that was God, made flesh in the womb of a Jewish maiden and laid to rest in a manger, because there was no room in the inn.

In the beginning, the earth was without form, and void. And darkness was upon the face of the deep. And the spirit of God moved upon the face of the waters.

And God said, Let there be light. Let the dry land appear. Let the earth bring forth grass. Let there be lights in the firmament. Let the waters bring forth abundantly the moving creature that hath life. Let the earth bring forth the living creature after his kind. Let us make man in our image.

In the beginning, God said. And it was so.

And God saw everything that he had made, and, behold, it was very good.

This is the end of my memoir about growing up gay in the Southern Baptist Church. It is not the end of the story.

EPILOGUE

THE KINGDOM OF HEAVEN

Died to self October 22, 2007.

It happened at the gym. I was sitting at the shoulder-press machine, resting between sets, when I suddenly felt excited. There was no reason to be excited. It had been a perfectly ordinary Monday. Nothing unusual had happened at work. I had no plans for the evening, nothing special scheduled for that week at all. Nevertheless, there it was—a bubble of energy welling up inside of me, rising up through my torso like the bubbles in a flute of champagne. It took only a few moments for it to complete its journey to the top of my head, and then it popped. The experience was very gentle. Only a few moments had gone by, but they were enough to change my experience of the world.

Perceptually, everything was as before. I was sitting on a bench, listening to pop music and watching the other people at the gym going from one machine to another. Yet something was different. Something was subtly but profoundly altered in the way the world appeared to me.

There was only one thing.

There was only one thing. I do not mean that there was only one thing and that I was sitting there looking at it. I mean that the people in the gym, the music, the weight machines, the air in the room, my breathing of the air, my body and my awareness were all one thing. I knew that if I were to have any thoughts, they would be that one thing as well.

But I did not have any thoughts, not for a while, though I cannot say how long I sat without thinking because time had suddenly stopped. I just looked around, not thinking anything, not making any demands on the moment, not doing anything. I understood, without having to think it, that everything that I was observing was myself. I understood that the other people and objects in the room were just as much myself as was my own body. Then the first thought arose. The first thought was this: "All of this is my mind." Those were the exact words that arose. Not "All of this is *in* my mind" or "All of this is *happening in* my mind," though I understood without thinking the thought that those things were true as well. But the startling truth of that moment was the realization that this one thing I had discovered was both the content and the structure of my mind, and that this mind was something much larger than I had ever previously suspected it might be.

The second thought that arose was this: who is this "my" that thinks it has a mind? Who is it that thinks there is anything it can possess? So I went looking for "my." I turned my attention in a direction that I had always thought of as inward and began a search for "my," for this self that thought it could possess something in a world where there was only one thing. In a world where there is only one thing, there is only one hiding place, and after I had looked behind and under and around it, the search for "my" was quickly over. I found nothing. No my, no I, no self—nothing. Michael Fields was gone. In his place, there was only awareness, a single point of awareness that was everywhere and everything. Everything I looked at shared equally in that awareness. Awareness was aware only of itself and only of that moment. It created that moment. Out of nothing. At the center of creation, at the center of awareness, what I found was nothing. At the center of creation, I found a void. Without actually thinking the thought, I tacitly understood that appearances to the contrary, the world around me, this one thing that was me, both did and did not exist.

Strangely enough, the discovery that I did not exist did not frighten me in the least. How could it? There was no "me" to be frightened, no "me" to be upset. I simply accepted the paradox that I could both not exist and yet still have sense experience and the occasional thought.

The next occasional thought was a question: "Aren't I supposed to be feeling something right now?" I had been around the block a few times on my spiritual quest and knew what was happening. I knew that I had just looked into the void, the famous No Thing at the heart of creation. So I wondered if I felt anything—bliss, ecstasy, nirvana—any of the feelings that are said to come at that moment. I was not aware of any feeling but went looking for one just the same, and this time I found something. I found a feeling that was very subtle and that at first I could not identify. As I sat with it longer, the word for the feeling arose: safe. I felt safe. Safe in a way I had never felt before. Safe because there was no me to be threatened. Safe because there was nothing out there that could threaten me because there was nothing else out there at all. Safe because there was no future to fear, no past to regret, safe because there was only one moment, only one place, only one thing, and I myself was that moment, that place and that thing.

"As it is above, so it is below, and as it is below, so it is above" runs the ancient occult dictum. Compare if you will my account of what happened at the gym with the following paragraph, taken from the first chapter of Lynne McTaggart's book *The Intention Experiment*:

> The double-slit experiment encapsulates the central mystery of quantum physics—the idea that a subatomic particle is not a single seat but the entire stadium. It also demonstrates the principle that electrons, which exist in a hermetic quantum state, are ultimately unknowable. You could not identify something about a quantum entity without stopping the particle in its tracks, at which point it would collapse to a single point.

As above, so below.

Among the many books in my apartment is a thin, tattered paperback called *The Zen Teachings of Huang Po.* I came across it not long ago while looking for another book. I had not opened the book in thirty-three years, not since Wes gave it to me in psychology class, just before I graduated from high school. I took the book down from the shelf, opened the brittle brown pages, and read the first paragraph. It made perfect sense. I continued to read. I read the whole book. Apart from some references to specific aspects of Buddhism, a religion about which I know only a little, the book made perfect sense. What I had once thought was Huang Po's deliberate attempt to make his words as obscure as possible turned out to be just the opposite. Huang Po was speaking as plainly as he could about a subject that, try as one might, cannot be put adequately into words.

> All the Buddhas and all sentient beings are nothing but the One Mind, beside which nothing exists. It is that which you see before you—begin to reason about it and you at once fall into error. It is like the boundless void that cannot be fathomed or measured. The One Mind alone is the Buddha.

The past does not exist. What exists are memories. Memories, like other thoughts, are real. They are actual things. That does not make them accurate or reliable, only real. The thought of the hamburger is a real thought. It is not a real hamburger.

The memory of trading comic books with one's friends is a real thought, but God only knows where the comic books are now. God knows because God's thoughts about things are the things themselves. God's memories are present realities. We may have memories of things past, but God's memories are the things themselves. Time past and time future are both present in the mind of God where Jesus and Nanny, Mama Fields and Bee Pa, Other Mother, Annelle, Ruth, Doug and Barnetta are present just as surely as my mother and father, my siblings and cousins, Beth, Steven, Kent and John are present, all present, all now in the mind of God, where all things are and which is all things. He's got the whole world in his hands.

Forty days and forty nights. The spirit of God moved the ark across the face of the waters that covered the world, the same water in which Cleopatra would one day bathe, the same water in which I would one day be baptized, the same water that tomorrow or the next day will fall as rain outside your window. The dove that brought a sign of dry land was sent out once again but never returned, would not be seen again until the day mankind wanted a new sign, the day John the Baptist lifted Jesus out of the River Jordan. God gave man a promise the day the boat settled on dry land: he would never again destroy the world with water. He made no mention of fire.

Forty days and forty nights. Dry land. The spirit of God drove Jesus into the wilderness where all that is not essential is burned away in the heat of the sun. What was left of Jesus in the starlit night? What was Jesus when he went into the desert, and what was he when he returned? What did he learn in the desert and, more to the point, what did he forget? What did Jesus become as one blistering day blurred into the next? And what did he cease to be?

Before there was Christianity, there was the Way. That is what Jesus's early followers called his teachings in the years immediately after his Crucifixion. Before there was Christianity, before there were Baptists or Southern Baptists, there was only the Way.

What Way did Jesus teach? What path through the wilderness is needed when the wilderness itself is a thought in the mind of God, where leaving happens the moment you arrive, where every starting point is as perfect as every destination, all present and perfect, all now in the mind of God, where all things are and which is all things?

The Way is not a path. It is the razor's edge. The Way is the moment-to-moment knowing that there is no place to go, that you are already complete and whole with the world around you.

Safe. The English word is derived from the Latin *salvus*, meaning "whole, intact, safe." So is our word "salvation." To be safe, to be saved, is to be whole. No sacrifice is necessary; no effort is needed to gain what is already yours. To be whole is to realize that the world is whole, the world is complete, just as it is, just as you are. Jesus walked out of the desert knowing one thing: the kingdom of heaven is spread out on the earth, in plain sight of everyone. It is that which you see before you. Jesus spent the rest of his short life spreading that good news. He walked from town to town teaching one thing: open your eyes. See it. See what the Buddha saw. See what Huang Po saw. See what Meher Baba saw. The kingdom of heaven is here now.

I was sitting at the shoulder-press machine, resting between sets. I did not really know how long I had been sitting there. Time had stopped. In a sense, I had been there an eternity, as eternity is simply what is left of the world when time and self are subtracted from it. A new thought arose: time to move. After all, I was at the gym. Soon someone would want to do shoulder presses. So I did what anyone who has just ceased to exist would do—I did the next thing. I finished my shoulder presses. I finished my workout. I left the gym, picked up a few things for dinner on my way home, ate dinner with my partner, read the paper, watched some television, went to bed, went to work the next day and the next, celebrated Thanksgiving, celebrated Christmas and got a promotion, each activity a thought arising in the void, each thought a petal in the thousand-petaled lotus floating in the darkness upon the face of the deep. One day a thought arose about a book that I would write.

Start again. At the beginning.

The kingdom of heaven is spread out on the earth.

The kingdom of heaven is here, the only place there is.

The kingdom of heaven is now, the only time there is.

The kingdom of heaven is this, the only thing there is.

The kingdom of heaven is this world.

It is this morning.

It is this thought.

It is this body.

It is this room.

It is this cabin where I write.

It is this window above the desk.

It is this forest outside the window.

It is this lake shimmering through the trees.

It is this chickadee perched on the branch.

It is this person who watches the bird.

This sunlight dancing on the water.

This music from the radio.

This dust mote in the air.

This air I breathe.

This, all of it, this.

This thought.

This air.

This sunlight.

This moment.

This.

This.

This.

ABOUT THE AUTHOR

Michael Fields was born and raised in Nashville, Tennessee. He is a graduate of Deep Springs College, Columbia University and the Fordham Graduate School of Social Service. He lives in New York City.

PERMISSIONS ACKNOWLEDGMENTS